Granville Carlyle Cuningham

A Scheme for Imperial Federation

A Senate for the Empire

Granville Carlyle Cuningham

A Scheme for Imperial Federation
A Senate for the Empire

ISBN/EAN: 9783337320829

Printed in Europe, USA, Canada, Australia, Japan

Cover: Foto ©Suzi / pixelio.de

More available books at **www.hansebooks.com**

A SCHEME
FOR
IMPERIAL FEDERATION,

A SENATE FOR THE EMPIRE

THREE ARTICLES REPRINTED
WITH ADDITIONS FROM 'THE WESTMINSTER REVIEW'
OF APRIL, JULY, AND OCTOBER, 1879

BY

GRANVILLE C. CUNINGHAM

OF MONTREAL, CANADA

WITH AN INTRODUCTION
BY
SIR FREDERICK YOUNG, K.C.M.G.

LONDON
LONGMANS, GREEN, AND CO.
AND NEW YORK
1895

All rights reserved

INTRODUCTION

When viewed from the national standpoint of the inestimable benefit of binding the Empire together in permanent union, no political subject is probably of greater and more supreme importance, and of wider interest to the whole British people, than the one which has received the comprehensive and expressive designation of 'Imperial Federation.' To the inquiry of what it is, I reply by answering in a sentence that it is the government of the Empire by the Empire for the Empire. The idea is not new. A hundred years ago Burke dreamed of its accomplishment, which in his own day appeared to be impracticable, owing to the physical impediments of distance, and the consequent impossibility of obtaining the necessary means of personal communication between the delegates of a Parliament which should comprise representatives of the Mother Country, and of our 'kith and kin' beyond the seas.

Since Burke's day, however, all the conditions which seemed to him to offer insuperable difficulties in this respect have been entirely changed. The great and glorious inventions of steam and telegraphy have annihilated distance, and brought the whole world into practical touch and instantaneous communication. In the latter decades of the nineteenth century we have no longer to encounter the objections which, in spite of his ardent advocacy of the advantages of the theory, seemed to the great orator of the past to frustrate any prospect of its being fulfilled.

Deeply imbued with the same patriotic sentiments as his own, realising the immense issues connected with this grand and noble conception, profoundly convinced of the vast benefit which would accrue to the British people if the principle of Imperial Federation could be fairly and thoroughly carried out, a few enthusiastic spirits among us have laboured earnestly for a quarter of a century in advocating it, and endeavouring to enlist the national sympathies, and to win in its favour the popular support.

My late lamented friend Mr. de Labilliere (all his life a warm and able advocate of Imperial Federation) published recently a book entitled 'Federal Britain.' In it he has given a very complete history of the rise and progress of the movement in favour of this great question from the year 1873 to the present time.

In the year 1876 I myself published a volume entitled 'Imperial Federation,' which contained a summary of my own views, by broadly advocating the 'principle' to be followed in dealing with it. From these views, I may say, I have never swerved. Time has only accentuated and confirmed in my own mind the opinion that they were based on a sound and correct conviction of the lines to be followed in developing the principle I then endeavoured to lay down.

Three years afterwards, in the year 1879, I received from a Canadian correspondent, Mr. Granville Cuningham, a series of most ably written articles, warmly supporting my own ideas on the subject, and developing in most full and comprehensive detail the plan by which, when once the principle of Imperial Federation, as already laid down by myself, was fully accepted, it could be successfully carried into effect. These articles I was able to get inserted in the 'Westminster Review,' through the favour of the then editor, the late Dr. Chapman. They were read with much interest, as indeed they deserved to be, by a limited circle of readers at the time.

Four years afterwards, in the year 1883, the Imperial Federation League was founded under the able leadership of its first president, the late Right Hon. W. E. Forster, M.P., who continued up to his death a most warm and energetic supporter of Imperial Federation, and by his wise counsel rendered invaluable help to a cause which he had so much at heart. He was succeeded by the Right Hon.

Edward Stanhope, M.P., in the presidential chair; and by Lord Rosebery: both showing an equally earnest interest in, and devoting much time and attention to, the question on behalf of which the League was founded.

For ten years the League lived and flourished, and succeeded in winning the adhesion of an increasing number of members, who showed their sympathy with its general objects by consenting to join it. But there is an old and trite saying, 'Many men, many minds.' While it is true, therefore, that, for a long while, harmonious action was maintained by the strenuous advocacy by its leaders, of the advantages of 'Imperial Federation,' *as a name*, whenever any question came to be touched upon, or discussed, as to the way in which it was to be carried into effect, great differences of opinion were developed among its members. Hence it became impossible to put forward publicly any plan with the seal and approval of the League as being its actual and definite programme of policy in detail for adoption. Of course, all the time there were active members of the League, like myself, who had our own plan 'cut and dried'; but this was only the individual, and not the collective, opinion of the League.

Meanwhile the inevitable and, in the opinion of some of us, the regrettable consequence of no detailed scheme of Imperial Federation having for many years been put forward by the League took place. It was constantly challenged—and this over and over again—by the organs of the Press, with having no feasible or practicable plan worthy of the name to put forward at all. The League was charged with being only a body of academical faddists and philosophical dreamers, and men desirous of making political capital, by superficially conjuring with a question possessing a grand and noble national name, without having any intention of grappling with it in reality, or probing its issues to its bottom depths. At length the League, after having accomplished a very important and most laudable and successful work, through the great influence its powerful organisation brought to bear, in enlightening the public mind as to its scope and object, was dissolved in the year 1893.

The Imperial Federation League has *come* and *gone*, but the *principle* on which it was founded remains deep down in the hearts of those who have always been its staunchest advocates. For the last two years efforts have been made to attempt to revive the League in some shape, under new auspices. While I am uncertain what particular line it may be thought fit to adopt, I cannot pledge myself to give to them my active support. They certainly, however, have my sympathy and good wishes, as having, I believe, an intention of going, in what I myself regard, in general terms, in a 'right direction.' However this may be, I have resolved, with the consent of Mr. Granville Cuningham, to republish the articles, to which I have referred, which appeared in the 'Westminster Review,' because they so entirely coincide, in their general application and intention, with my own original views of Imperial Federation.

To these views I have always firmly adhered from the first, because I believe they contain the germ and gist of the realisation of this grand national political problem, for the successful accomplishment of which I have worked so earnestly for so many years of my life.

FREDERICK YOUNG.

5 Queensberry Place, S.W.:
  October, 1895.

A SCHEME
FOR
IMPERIAL FEDERATION

CHAPTER I

THE attention of the British public has of late been directed to the question of the Federation of the Empire by various discussions that have taken place at meetings of the Royal Colonial Institute, by the publication of a volume on Imperial Federation by Mr. (now Sir) Frederick Young, and by the appearance in leading periodicals of articles dealing with the matter. It is not, however, pretended that, though attention has been directed to the question, public interest in it has been evoked to any large extent. As a rule, the British public is supremely indifferent to Colonial affairs. Probably not one man out of a hundred of what are called the educated classes is at all conversant with the salient features of any of the Colonies, could give more than the roughest sketch of the geographical peculiarities, or even an outline of the social, political, and economic characteristics of the country. Those few who do know anything of the Colonies are generally either those who have friends resident in them or who have business relations with them which necessitate some knowledge of Colonial affairs. Nor is the reason of this indifference far to seek or difficult to understand. To the individual Briton the Colonies are totally uninteresting, because he has no immediate interests bound up in them; and to the British public collectively they are totally uninteresting, because they in no direct way affect the wealth or strength of England. As the result of this feeling we have the fact that many of the leading minds of England would be in favour of allowing the Colonies to drift asunder from the Mother Country, that most would be inclined to allow matters to go on as at present, and that few, if any, would favour such changes in the system of governing as would draw the connection more closely.

Recognising such a condition of things,

the reader may perhaps ask, 'What good can be gained by discussing the question of the Federation of the Empire?' It is the aim of the following pages to answer this question, and to show that in the future the welfare of England and her Colonies must be interdependent. Hitherto, as the Empire has grown, the political system of the Empire has remained stationary. The acquisition of new territory and the gradual growth of additional peoples and societies has not been accompanied by a similar growth and development of the political system of the Empire. To draw a parallel from animal life, we may say that, while the limbs and various parts of the organism have developed to a prodigious extent, the cerebro-spinal centre has remained the same. In other words, the Empire of Britain, as we see it to-day, consists of the Mother Country, and an appendage of loosely-connected States in various conditions of dependence, or rather independence. And perhaps not the least curious fact in this connection is that those States that are the largest, wealthiest, most populous, and most likely to be of value to the Mother Country are precisely those that are most independent. And there can be no doubt that under the present political system of the Empire this independence of each Colony will increase with its wealth and population. It cannot be otherwise. Undoubtedly there exists in the Colonies a very strong sentiment of affection and love to the Mother Country, which has held them together, and will continue to hold them long after a consideration of material interests would advise a different course. There is more of an Imperial feeling, and more love for the ideal Empire among Colonists than is to be found in the Mother Country. Colonists are proud of being British subjects; they are proud of the historical traditions of England, proud of her freedom, of her statesmen, of her literature, of her wealth, and deeply loyal to her Queen. It must not be forgotten, too, that to a very great number of Colonists there is some one 'little green spot' of the old country that is particularly dear and sacred, if not from personal recollection, then by tradition as the place where 'father was born,' or where 'mother' lived before she 'came out,' or perhaps where the more pretentious 'family' originally came from. All these and kindred sentiments are important factors, as helping to maintain the connection between the Colonies and the old country, and only those who know the Colonies can know how important these factors are. The English public is very apt to look upon Colonists as to a certain extent foreigners, and to lose sight of the fact that they are in reality just such as they are themselves—sprung from the same stock, inheriting the same traditions, and animated with the same national spirit. But no matter how strong these sentiments and feelings may be, it must be borne in mind that after all they are only sentiments, and in the natural course of affairs, when the material interests of the Colony run counter to these sentiments, it cannot be otherwise but that these sentiments should give way. As pointed out above, I believe that the sentimental regard of the Colonies for the Mother Country, the love of Colonists for the ideal Empire, is so strong that material interests will frequently be sacrificed to this feeling, the connection between the Colonies and the Mother Country being maintained long after a thoroughly dispassionate view of the case would recommend separation. But as the development of nations goes on there must ultimately be reached a point when the tension becomes too great to be borne; when the sentimental feelings will be more than counterbalanced by the material interests; when to maintain the connection would mean ruin and misery for the Colony, while separation would bring wealth and happiness. Let us state a case exemplifying this.

In all likelihood within the next fifty years the population of Canada will have grown to twenty-five or thirty millions. There will have been, of course, a concomitant increase in the wealth of the country. Is it possible that Canada will then be able to stand in the position that she now holds towards England? In the event of England's going to war with any Continental nation Canada would immediately become an object for the attack of that nation; she would require to defend herself; to plunge into all the heavy expenditure required in modern warfare, and would become liable to devastation and pillage, and all this, not from any quarrel of her own, not because she had decided to go into war, but simply because she is part of the British Empire. Or again, we might easily conceive the position to be reversed: that some foreign Power had not observed a certain treaty; that the infraction of this treaty affected Canadian interests very much more than English interests; that England refused to enforce observance of the treaty; and as Canada is a Colony without power either to make treaties or to enforce their observance, Canada would simply have to sacrifice her interests and submit to whatever the loss or humiliation might be in order to maintain the connection with the Mother Country. But is it reasonable to suppose that a country wealthy and powerful as Canada would be under this supposititious case could exist in a position so dangerous to her well-being and so humiliating to her *amour-propre*? We think not; and we think it will be equally clear to any one who will realise to himself the position supposed that Canada would be impelled to follow one of two courses, either to obtain adequate representation in the councils of the Empire, or to become entirely separated from the Empire. As a development of the present Colonial policy the latter is the only course that would be possible.

Indeed, without looking so far into the future, as in the above case, we think it will become apparent, on considering the Colonial policy of the Empire, that growth and development of the Colony can result only in separation from the Mother Country. The various stages in the political growth of a Colony are somewhat as follows :—In the first instance we have a governor appointed by her Majesty, assisted by a council of three or four members, probably the heads of the naval and military force stationed at the place, and who are members *ex-officio*. In the next stage the council is augmented by the addition of a few local men also appointed by her Majesty. As the Colony grows the people are granted the privilege of electing some members of the council—perhaps about a third of the entire number—the remainder being appointed by her Majesty. At a further stage a legislative assembly is added, entirely elected by the people, with a council, partly elected and partly nominated as a second chamber; and the fully-developed stage is reached when we have both chambers elected by the people (with a difference in the franchise), and the Government carried on by a governor (appointed by her Majesty), and a cabinet composed of members of either of the legislative chambers; or we have, as in Canada, a House of Commons elected by the people, and a Senate Chamber, nominated by the governor in council, constituting the Parliament, the council being the Government of the day, and composed of members of the Senate and Parliament similar to the Government of England. In these various stages we may see that the direction of the growth of the political system of the Colony is towards a system that will be perfect in itself, apart from any other political system of the Empire. There is no tendency for the political system of the Colony to become ultimately embraced in the political system of the Mother Country. Quite otherwise. The channel of communication between the two, and the official representation of the one to the other is absolutely the same in the first stage as in the last, and is relatively much smaller and more imperfect in the last stage than in the first. The little desert rock in mid-ocean and the vast territory containing many provinces are on the same footing as regards representation in the Imperial Parliament: for the one as for the other the only official channel is through a governor in communication with the Colonial Secretary. The inconveniences arising from this want of representation have been felt, and it has been attempted to obviate them by the appointment of an 'agent' for the Colony, one who represents some English or Scotch constituency in the House, and who undertakes also to advocate the cause and represent the views of some particular Colony. Such representation as this, however, is of but little value, as the agent is not responsible to the Colony (in a political sense), and merely renders his services in consideration of his salary. Nor can the expression of his sentiments have much weight in the House. He may be able to afford interesting information in regard to the Colony he represents; but on any question arising on which a vote might be taken, he would be bound to vote in accordance with the interests of the constituency he represented, and not in accordance with the interests of the Colony, should these interests at the time be different. In like manner the formation of an advisory board, composed of Colonial representatives that should advise the Colonial Secretary on matters affecting the Colonies, as proposed by Sir Julius Vogel (in the 'Nineteenth Century' for July, 1877), is open to grave objections. It would be a feature out of harmony with the principle of government by elected representatives; it is difficult to see how such a board could be politically responsible to the Colonies it represented, and it is still more difficult to see how such a board could exert any influence over the

Colonial Secretary in the event of his choosing to disregard its advice. Indeed, Sir Julius Vogel himself proposes such a board as a merely temporary arrangement, recognising the fact that perfect representation of the Colonies can only be effected by the popular election of men to serve in the Imperial Parliament. But representation of the Colonies in the present Parliament of England would not be beneficial. The greater number of the measures brought before the House of Commons is of a purely local nature, and it would be quite out of place that Colonial representatives should have a voice in the discussion of these. The only chamber to which Colonial representatives could be admitted, and in which their presence would be desirable, would be one in which the matters deliberated upon were as distinct from the local affairs of the Mother Country as they were distinct from the local affairs of the Colonies. It must be the supreme chamber of the Empire; the apex of the political system to which all the lower chambers must lead up. But of such a chamber there is not as yet even the germ. There has been no attempt made, and there seems to be no desire to make the attempt, to separate local from Imperial affairs in English parliamentary government. The present Parliament of England is nominally the chief chamber of the Empire, and this Parliament, with regard to the rest of the Empire, can be looked upon as none other than a local parliament. By no expedient short of representation by election could a chamber be constituted that would afford adequate representation to the Colonies; such a chamber means the formation of an Imperial Parliament in which all parts of the Empire would be represented, while to local parliaments would be relegated the local affairs of the various localities. In another chapter I shall discuss more fully the relative positions of the Imperial and local parliaments, but in the meantime it may be well to point out here how the establishment of this Parliament would concentrate the whole vast Empire in one chamber. As each Colony grew and developed, it would not grow as now towards independence and rivalry of the Mother Country, but simply towards representation in the Imperial Parliament. When it became sufficiently large and important, it would be admitted into the federation of the Empire. Its representatives would have their proportionate share in moulding the policy of the Empire, and its population would contribute a proportionate share towards maintaining the Empire. The Mother Country and the Colony would eventually gain strength and support, the one from the other. Now, the Colony is a present source of weakness and expense, and a future source of rivalry to the Mother Country, while the Mother Country, after a certain stage of growth has been reached by the Colony, ceases to be any support, and may become a source of danger and disaster to the Colony.

Though the formation of such a Federal Parliament is new to England it is quite in accordance with the political genius of the Empire. In the dominion of Canada now may be seen a system of confederation such as would be applicable to the whole Empire. Here in each province, Ontario, Quebec, New Brunswick, Nova Scotia, Prince Edward Island, Manitoba, and British Columbia, there is a local parliament under a lieutenant-governor entrusted with the management of the local affairs; while, embracing all these, and composed of men from all these provinces, there is the Dominion Parliament to which is entrusted the management of general or Dominion matters. There is in the nor'-west an example of the undeveloped province too small to enjoy representation by election, but

under the government of a lieutenant-governor
and a nominated council. To parallel this
system in the Empire at large we should have
a local parliament for England (Scotland and
Ireland also if need be), local parliaments for
some Colonies, a governor and council for
others, while over all and superior to all would
be the Federal Parliament, composed of men
elected from Great Britain and such of the
Colonies as had grown to sufficient size and
importance. Under such a supreme chamber
the growth and development of each Colony
would culminate in representation in that
chamber. Under the present system the
growth and development of each Colony can
culminate only in separation from the Mother
Country. And we think it is the intuitive perception of this fact that accounts chiefly for
the indifference of Englishmen to the growth
of the Colonies.

That the development of the Colony is
paralleled by its tendency to separate from, and
become independent of, the Mother Country
we have many evidences constantly coming
forward around us. The establishment of the
Supreme Court of Canada may be taken as
one of these. In this case it was found absolutely necessary for the material interests of

the country to establish a supreme court in the country, from whose decisions there should be no appeal to any other tribunal. The right of appeal to the Judicial Committee of the Privy Council was found to be fraught with so many inconveniences and burdened with so heavy a cost that it was a right only to be enjoyed by the richer classes, and a threat of an appeal to this court would be sufficient to make a man of limited means give up his case rather than incur what must necessarily be a very heavy outlay. The establishment of the Supreme Court of Canada was the outcome of a popular necessity, as it was found practically impossible to carry on the judicial system without it. But what is the result of this? It separates the judicial system of the Colony from that of the Mother Country; it is but one step on the road towards the disintegration of the Empire; and though as yet the separation is not complete, as there remains still the right of appealing either to the Judicial Committee or to the Supreme Court of Canada, yet there can be no doubt that as the country develops and grows, even this modification will be removed and the right confined to the Supreme Court of Canada. The same necessities that called the court into being in the first instance will ultimately bar the right of appeal to the Privy Council.[1]

Again, in the military system of the developed Colony we find the disintegrating forces at work. In Canada the whole burden of the military system is now borne by the Colony. The troops that have to be maintained, and which number about 30,000 men (in 1875 number of militia trained 28,845), are maintained entirely by the Colony. There are still some two regiments of Imperial troops retained in Halifax, but these, as Sir Francis Hincks has shown ('Nineteenth Century' for May, 1878), are so retained to subserve an Imperial necessity, and for the convenience of the Imperial authorities, and not for the purpose of defending the Colony. Of course we do not contend that the troops required for Canada should be maintained in any other manner but by the Colony, so long as the existing Imperial policy obtains. It would be absurd to expect that the British taxpayer should pay for troops to garrison and support a Colony from which he neither nationally nor

---

[1] The right of appeal from the Supreme Court of Canada to the Judicial Committee of the Privy Council has been established, with this modification, that after a case has been heard by the Supreme Court leave has to be obtained to appeal to the Privy Council (G. C. C., 1895).

personally derives any benefit, and particularly when the Colony is quite able and willing to assume this expense herself. Colonists see this at once, and willingly assume the burden of the military expense. The result of this is immediate and direct. The Imperial and Colonial military systems are completely separated. There is established in the Colony an army of trained soldiers that will grow with the growth of the Colony, and which in another fifty years may, and probably will, attain to a very large size, and which army is entirely beyond Imperial control, and may be used for any purpose. We do not here mean to hint, as the words might imply, that there is even the remotest likelihood of the army being used to fight against the Mother Country. Knowing the intense loyalty to the Mother Country that exists in the Colonies, it is more than probable that the first great war in which the Colonial army will see service will be in the defence or assistance of the Mother Country. The offer of Canadian troops to assist England in the event of an Anglo-Russian war bears out this view; but it also incidentally shows how complete already is the separation of the Imperial and Colonial military systems. The offer comes to England more like the offer of assistance from a foreign Power than as the due and proper help which should come from all parts of the Empire if the Empire were truly one. The very outburst of applause which this offer called forth from the press of England really shows how unexpected it was, and how spontaneous and uncalled-for it was. England had no *right* to expect it; she had no *right* to ask for it; it was the outcome of the intensely loyal and affectionate sentiment that exists in Canada towards the Mother Country.

But from this will it be maintained that Canada will always be ready and willing to plunge into the horrors of war to gratify this sentiment? Canada will derive neither honour nor glory for herself from such wars; she has no voice either to approve or disapprove such wars; and even though she were reimbursed for the use of her troops by the Home Government, at the end of such a struggle she would find herself *minus* many valuable citizens, and much property that no money could compensate, and *plus*—nothing. Lord Blachford has said ('Nineteenth Century' for October, 1877) that he believes that the Colonies would plunge into one such war as this, but would shrink from a second, and we think in this view he is correct. Nor is such a course on the part of the Colonies to be wondered at. As matters stand at present the mere fact of the Colonies being nominally part of the Empire of Britain renders them liable to attack, and marks them out as proper and legitimate prey for any Power with which England may go to war. Even though the Colony did not actively take part in the war by sending her troops to assist the Imperial troops, yet she would be forced to take part in it, in so far as it would be necessary for her to be prepared to defend herself from the probable attacks of the Power with which England was at war. The fact of England's declaring war would necessitate that every Colony that was worth attacking should immediately put itself upon a war footing. Hitherto no evil results of much magnitude have followed from this position; but this has been, not because this danger did not exist, but because at the time of the former wars of England none of the Colonies was worth attacking. But this will not always be the case. Canada twenty-five years ago was poor and insignificant in comparison with her present condition, and the growth in wealth, population, and power in future years will be even more rapid than in the past. To put the case, as we stated it before, when the population has increased to some thirty millions, as in all likelihood it will within the next fifty years, with the corresponding growth in wealth that this population implies, would any one maintain that it would then be to her interest to continue in the position which she now holds in regard to the Mother Country? Nay, would any one maintain that it would be possible for her to continue in such a position? The fact that she might at any time be attacked in order to strike at England, the fact that she would be powerless to employ diplomacy to avert such attacks, that she must simply drift with the stream, no matter what resulted, the feeling of vagueness, uncertainty, and helplessness that would result, would produce a state of tension and irritation that would be intolerable, and that no sentimental feeling, however strong, could overbalance. The general good would require the adoption of some measures that would put the country in a clear and definite position before the world. Either she must become truly one with the Empire of Britain, with the proper voice and weight in the councils of the Empire that this oneness infers, or she must cease to be part of the Empire. We do not think that, ultimately, there can be any *via media* between these two courses, and under the present political system the latter is the only course that would be possible. No doubt before this ultimate position was reached intermediate positions would be adopted to smooth over difficulties as they arose, but it must be admitted that the position to which the Colonies are drifting, considering the military aspect of the case, and under the present political system of the Empire, is that of complete separation from the Mother Country.

Again, there is a tendency towards separation when we consider the treaty-making power. Under the present Imperial political system, a Colony has no power to make treaties with other nations; no matter how immediately and deeply her interests may be affected, she can only make treaties with other nations through the Imperial authorities, and the only official channel of communication with the Imperial powers is through the governor, in communication with the Colonial Secretary. For the small and undeveloped Colony this is sufficient. Her local interests occupy so small and insignificant a position in the international questions of great Powers that any Imperial treaty completely ignores such interests. As the Colony grows, however, local interests grow in importance, and ultimately thrust themselves forward as factors that cannot be ignored. The Colonists feel that in the making of treaties in which the vital interests of the Colony are largely affected, it is absolutely necessary for the well-being of the community that those interests should be properly represented and advocated, and they can only be so represented by men whose personal interests are bound up with the Colony—that is, by Colonists. Colonists would feel it as an intolerable injustice if a treaty should be drawn up with a neighbouring Power which would materially affect their personal well-being without any reference being made to themselves in the matter. No doubt such injustice has been done in times past, and has been submitted to, while the Colony was too insignificant to bring pressure upon the Mother Country. But with the growth of the Colony there comes a time when such injustice would produce a strain that might cause rupture. The Mother Country sees this, and temporarily smooths over the difficulty by allowing Colonial representatives to have a seat at the treaty board.

Here, again, however, these representatives are admitted more as the plenipotentiaries of a foreign Power than as representatives who have an inherent right to be heard—the right of all parts of the Empire to have a voice in the governing of the Empire. And this principle of representation by plenipotentiaries being once granted and adopted, we think it will be admitted that the weight and effect of such representation will be proportionate to the importance of the Colony, and that as the Colony develops a larger share will be claimed in the making of treaties in which the Colonial interests are at stake, the final stage of which development is, when the Colony claims the right to make treaties without reference to the Mother Country, and this means separation. There are many practical examples that could be cited, and which will occur to many, of the growth of this principle of representation by plenipotentiaries. Thus, at the time of the drawing up of the Ashburton Treaty in 1834, which lost to Canada greater part of the State of Maine, Canada, or, more properly, New Brunswick, was unrepresented at the treaty board, except through her governor, in correspondence with the Colonial Secretary, and there can be little doubt that the blunders and injustice committed by that treaty were mainly traceable to the want of proper representation of the local interests of the Colony. Again, at the drawing up of the Treaty of Washington in 1872, in which the question of the Canadian Fisheries was involved, we find that local interests had so grown in importance that they could no longer be overlooked by the Imperial authorities, and Canada was represented by a plenipotentiary appointed by the Canadian Government whose special mission it was to advocate the proper recognition of Canadian interests. Still more was this principle recognised in the appointment of the Halifax Commission which sat in 1877 to decide the Canadian Fisheries question, where Canada had an equal voice with England and the United States, and a largely preponderating influence when we consider the appointment of counsel. It is not a little significant, too, that in this last case, the only international tribunal at which Canadian interests have been adequately represented by Canadian representatives, the decision for the first time in any dispute, as between Canada and the United States, was favourable to Canada, thus emphasising the value of due representation of local interests in the settlement of Imperial questions.

Thus we see that with an increase in the

wealth and population of a Colony, there goes a corresponding decrease in the strength of the ties to the Mother Country. Instead of an expansion of the political system of the Mother Country that would embrace the Colony, there is a development of the political system of the Colony that renders it independent of the Mother Country. And this separation does not arise from a desire on the part of the Colonies to be separate from the Mother Country, nor yet from a desire on the part of the Mother Country to throw off the Colonies, but is simply the only possible result that can follow under the present political system of the Empire. Under the present system there is no possibility of a true extension of the Empire. England may acquire Colonies, as she has done, and hold them for a time, but the growth and development of these Colonies must be continuous steps towards separation. As the foregoing analysis we think has shown, their ultimate development, considered under various aspects, means complete separation from the Mother Country. At no stage in the political life of the Colony is there any tendency to become merged in the political life of the Empire at large, but at every stage we can mark a step towards separation from the

Mother Country. Nor can it be otherwise. The political genius of the Anglo-Saxon races requires that the government should be carried on by the representatives of the people elected by the people. But there is no room for the representation of the Colonies under the present Imperial system. To add Colonial members to the present English House of Commons, and to require men from various far distant parts of the Empire to vote and spend their time in listening to debates upon all the local matters belonging to England, Scotland, and Ireland, would be absurd. Equally absurd is it to imagine that the present House of Commons of Great Britain can ever be the true Parliament of the Empire, the chamber in which would be found the concentrated opinion and will of the Empire. A parallel to this might be seen if it were attempted to make the local Legislative Assembly of Ontario, containing only representatives of Ontario, the Parliament of the Dominion of Canada; or if it were attempted to make the local Legislative Assembly of the State of New York, containing only representatives from the State of New York, the Congress for the United States of America. But just as in the Dominion of Canada there is one Dominion Parliament superior to the local legislatures and containing representatives from all the provinces in the Dominion, and just as in the United States of America there is one chief Congress superior to all the State assemblies and containing representatives from all the States of the Union, so in the British Empire—if the Empire is ever to be truly one—there must be a chief Parliament of the Empire, superior to all the local parliaments of the various countries, provinces, and Colonies composing the Empire, and containing representatives from various parts of the Empire. We cannot see that any scheme short of this would be in accord with the political genius of the peoples composing the Empire. We do not mean that every Colony, great or small, as we find them at present, should be at once given representation in the Imperial Parliament, but that as each Colony grows in strength and importance, it should ultimately be granted such representation, and thus be embraced in the Empire. Any Imperial system of governing that lacks this fundamental principle of representation of the Colonies in the chief Parliament of the Empire contains the germ which, when developed, must break up the Empire ; and, however great may be the difficulties in the way of forming this chief Parliament, we must either deal with these difficulties, or accept the alternative of seeing in the near future the Empire of Britain broken up, and the present Colonies constituted as independent and powerful nations.

Before closing this chapter I will briefly sketch the condition of the Empire under one chief Imperial Parliament, and point out some of the changes that would be necessary if the federation of the Empire were ever to be an accomplished fact. The one great principle which must form the groundwork of the required changes is the separation of local from national or Imperial interests. In a truly unified Empire the Imperial Parliament should be entirely superior to the local affairs of any one part of the Empire. The local affairs of Great Britain should have no more place in the Imperial Parliament than have the local affairs of Canada or Australia. The Imperial Parliament should deal only with the affairs of the Empire at large. In the so-called Imperial Parliament at present, however, it is far otherwise, more than two-thirds of the measures dealt with having reference to purely local matters, in which the rest of the Empire is no more interested than the people of England would be interested in the extension of the water-system of the City of Winnipeg. The first change would be the separation of local affairs from Imperial affairs, and this could only be effected by the formation of local parliaments for Great Britain and Ireland. To these parliaments should be left the management of all local business, such as education, sanitary inspection, railway regulation, liquor questions, licensing, traffic laws, and all the hundred and one other local matters that at present clog the machinery of the Imperial Parliament. These parliaments would be under a lieutenant-governor, or viceroy (as in Ireland), who would be appointed by the Queen, with the advice of her ministers, these ministers being chosen from the Imperial Parliament. The Imperial Parliament would deal with all international, inter-colonial, and Imperial matters. It would be composed of men sent from various parts of the Empire, and would be formed on the same principles as at present. As the local affairs of Great Britain and Ireland would no longer have a place in this chamber, it would be unnecessary to have so complete a representation of each locality, and therefore the number of members might be considerably less than at present, and still leave an adequate representation of England, Scotland, and Ireland, and a proper preponderance over the Colonial members.

Under such a parliament as this the whole Empire would be held together. This would be the central point from which would emanate the supreme controlling force to every part of the Empire. To this parliament every Colony as it grew in wealth and strength would bring its support and health. England would not then look with an indifferent eye at the growth of the Colonies, but their development and extension would be of as immediate importance to her as is the development of the wealth of an English county. The Empire of Britain would then truly be an 'Empire on which the sun never sets,' and an Empire vast and powerful such as the sun never shone on before. Boundless resources would be contained within herself, every conceivable want could be supplied from her own territory, while at the same time she would have at her call armies so vast that the whole world would stand in awe of the might of England. For such results as these would it not be desirable to carry out a federation of the Empire?

In another chapter I hope to be able to show, from an economical point of view, the practical benefit that would result both to England and the Colonies from the adoption of a federal system.

CHAPTER II

SOME ten years ago, if we remember rightly, Mr. John Bright made a series of vigorous speeches embodying advice and counsel to the working classes of Great Britain. He pointed out to them the mistake they were committing in crowding into cities and engaging in mechanical and manufacturing work, to the neglect of agriculture. The burden of his advice was: 'Go back to the land.' He pointed out how much of the land of Great Britain and Ireland was still lying waste: held as deer forests and grouse moors, which, if cultivated, would maintain directly many thousands, and the produce of which would cheapen the necessaries of life to many thousands more who worked in cities. He even propounded a scheme for purchasing these waste lands from their present proprietors at compulsory rates, in order to give them back to the people.

No doubt Mr. Bright was right in the

advice he gave, and much of the forcing of trade and over-production of manufactures which has resulted in the present commercial stagnation and disorganisation of the labour market, would have been avoided had the mass of the people gone back to the land. He clearly foresaw the dangers that lay ahead, and he rightly pointed out the safe course to be followed. The error that he fell into was in directing the people to the uncultivated lands of Great Britain, as though these were the only uncultivated lands that the Empire possessed. Though these lands are waste lands in an agricultural sense, they are not so from an æsthetic or even an economic point of view. They are the recreation grounds of the wealthy classes of the Empire, and are for this reason of high value. To take these lands in a compulsory manner from their owners and split them up into farms would create evils far greater than would be cured by that process. It would disorganise rather than consolidate society. The lands to which the people should go are not the parks and pleasure-grounds of Old England, but the waste lands of the outlying parts of the Empire. When there are thousands of acres of magnificent land lying unoccupied and unused, waiting, as it were, to be cultivated to yield ample sustenance for vast populations, why interfere with the rights of property of a very large class of the community by such a measure as compulsory purchase? These outlying parts are the true waste lands of the Empire, and it is to these lands that the people should be directed. It seems absurd that, in an Empire such as that of Britain, it should be deemed necessary to propound any such scheme as that of purchasing the deer parks and grouse moors of Great Britain for the purpose of cultivation, while vast tracts of better land in neighbouring parts of the Empire are left waste and totally unoccupied. Suppose, for example, that in the county of Kent there could not be found land enough for all those resident there who were willing and anxious to engage in agriculture, while in Yorkshire there were vast tracts of cultivable land *unowned* and unoccupied: would it not be the wiser policy to encourage the people of Kent to move to Yorkshire and take up land there, rather than to attempt to make room for them in Kent by the compulsory purchase of the parks and flower gardens of the wealthier residents? Yet the same in kind, though differing in degree, is the policy that would devise the compulsory purchase of the deer parks and grouse moors of Great Britain, while in Canada, Australia, New Zealand, and various other parts of the Empire there are vast tracts of unoccupied land, capable of absorbing ten hundred times the surplus population of Great Britain. Surely it would be the better policy to direct the people to these lands.

But if the pressure of population in Great Britain were to be relieved by encouraging emigration to the Colonies, how would this benefit England? Under the present Colonial policy emigration to the Colonies means the permanent loss to England of so many people. When an emigrant leaves her shores he ceases to be available for her defence, and he is no longer taxable for her support. His departure certainly tends to reduce the burden of poor rates, and by his productive labour in the new land whither he has gone he tends to cheapen the cost of the staple necessaries of life in England. But these effects would be produced quite as much whether he went to Canada or to the United States : whether he went to another part of the Empire or to a foreign country. The fact that he leaves England is the only fact in which England is interested: where he goes to is of but little consequence, as in any case he is lost to England. In this way he differs from the labourer who moves from Kent to Yorkshire, under the supposititious case stated, for this migration does not reduce the population of the nation, and directly increases the national wealth, in consequence of the labour becoming more productive. The emigrant who goes to the Colonies tends by his labour to develop and enrich the Colony. And under the present system of governing the Empire the growth and development of a Colony can only result in separation from the Mother Country. I have already pointed out that under the present Imperial policy every stage of development in the life of a Colony is an approach towards separation from the Mother Country. There is no possibility of the Colony being ultimately embraced by the political system of the Mother Country. Thus every emigrant who leaves the Mother Country and seeks a new home in a Colony, enriches and develops that Colony by his labour; by his labour he helps to found what in the near future will be an independent rival nation. It is in this particular that the great difference lies between the labourer who moves to

Yorkshire and he who moves to Canada; and it is the intuitive perception of this state of things that has always rendered England so indifferent to the direction of the stream of emigration—nay, has frequently made England desirous of entirely stopping the stream. If the Empire were truly one, would not the growth and development of any Colony be of the most vital importance to England? If Canada were as much a part of the Empire as is Scotland, would it not be England's first care to direct the stream of emigration to Canada rather than allow it to go to the States? In a truly unified Empire the farmer in Kent and the farmer in Manitoba would be equally subjects of the Empire: the one as the other would be liable for her defence, taxable for her support, and by his labour help to increase the national wealth. Such a position as this, however, could only be realised under a federation of the Empire, which would accord similar political privileges to each, similar responsibilities, and similar representation in the Imperial Parliament. Under such a system emigration to the Colonies would no longer be looked upon as a loss of population to the nation, the emigrant would still remain truly one of the nation, his labour while enriching the district whither he went would also enrich the Empire at large; his transference from one part where his labour was not required, and where his support was a burden on the community, to another part of the Empire where his labour was of high value, and where he was self-supporting, would convert him from an 'unproductive consumer' to a producer. Under a federal system it would be England's aim to encourage emigration from the Mother Country to the Colonies, so as to enhance the producing power of each individual of the nation—in other words, to increase the national wealth.

A glance at the emigration statistics for the last half century will show how little directive control has been exercised over emigration. Thus, in the sixty-two years from 1815 to 1876 the total number of emigrants who left the United Kingdom was 8,424,942. Their destinations were as follows:—

United States	5,467,075
British North America	1,549,010
Australasia	1,165,628
Other places	243,229
	8,424,942

Thus, while England sent 5,467,075 emigrants to develop and enrich a foreign Power, she secured only 2,957,867 for her own Colonies, assuming that the other places are British possessions.

Taking the money value of these emigrants at 1,000 dollars apiece, as is ordinarily assumed in the United States, we find that they represent a sum of 5,467,075,000 dollars, or about 1,125,000,000*l*. sterling, that England has presented to the United States. This, spread over a period of sixty-two years, represents an annual gift of nearly 19,000,000*l*. sterling. Is it surprising that, under such a system of assistance, the United States should have prospered and grown at a rate that has amazed the world? This immense stream of emigration might, with the exertion of very little directive force, have been used for the fertilising of the British Colonies. The Colonies are capable of absorbing ten times this number and yet have room for more. The money value of these Colonists would have been added to the national wealth of Britain, instead of having been handed over to a foreign Power. But, doubtless, the reason of the indifference to the destination of emigrants from England is to be found in the fact that, under the present Colonial policy, the development of the Colonies means ultimately separation from the Mother Country, and it is felt that it matters little whether emigrants go directly to a foreign Power or to a part of the Empire which will ultimately, and chiefly by reason of the accession of these very emigrants, become a foreign Power. Perhaps it may even be argued that it is better to let these emigrants go to a foreign Power that is already established rather than to direct them to the Colonies where they will in the near future found other independent nations.

If England were independent of other countries, if she could supply the daily wants of her inhabitants from her own territory, if she could absorb the manufactures of her inhabitants within her own territory, one could understand and appreciate the Colonial policy that has hitherto been adopted by the Home Government. But when England is dependent on other countries for the bare necessaries of life, when she is dependent on foreign countries for a market for her manufactured goods, one cannot but be amazed at the policy that would advise indifference to emigration; at the policy that has for its result the loss of the Colonies; the loss, in other words, of those very lands which, if peopled with the emigrants from Great Britain, could supply all the necessaries of life to, and afford a market to absorb all the manufactures of, England.

A few figures will show to what a large extent England is dependent on outside countries for the necessaries of life. Thus, the home-grown wheat crop of 1878, which was reported to be a full average, amounted to 11,500,000 quarters. And in order to supply the home market 13,000,000 quarters would have to be imported from abroad.[1] In other words, England could supply less than one-half of the wheat required to support her population. And it cannot be expected that there can in the future be much material increase in the quantity of wheat grown in the United Kingdom. Indeed, the tendency seems to be rather in the opposite direction, as from agricultural statistics it appears that, whereas in 1870 there were (in the United Kingdom) 3,773,663 acres under wheat, in 1876 there were only 3,125,342 acres thus occupied, being a decrease of 648,321 acres. In 1877 again the acreage was about 3,300,000, and in 1878 about 3,400,000.[2]

[1] In 1891 the home grown wheat crop was 9,342,840 quarters, while the wheat and wheat-flour imported amounted to 82,359,776 cwt., or about 21,000,000 quarters (G. C. C., 1895).

[2] In 1891 the total acreage under wheat in the United Kingdom had decreased to 2,388,661 (G. C. C., 1895).

A comparison of the values of food imports for the years 1870 and 1876 shows how startlingly large is the sum that England pays to other countries for the common necessaries of life, and how rapidly this sum is increasing. The following table gives the values of the various articles imported in the respective years [1]:—

	1870	1876
	£	£
Foreign stock (live and dead)	7,656,606	19,030,455
Corn, flour, and grain of all kinds	34,054,657	51,534,648
Butter	6,793,877	9,702,624
Cheese	3,274,331	4,251,428
Eggs	1,102,080	2,610,231
	52,881,551	87,129,386

In 1877 the total value of the above articles imported was 96,879,737l., the value under the heading 'corn, flour, &c.,' having risen to 63,192,224l.

Taking the population of the United Kingdom at the following figures:—

1870	31,205,000
1876	33,093,000
1877	33,446,000

we find the value of the above food importa-

[1] The value of foreign food imported, embracing a more extensive list of articles than that given in the text, has risen from 121,143,798l. in 1876, to 151,288,783l. in 1891. See *Whitaker's Almanack*, 1895 (G. C. C.).

tions per head of the population to be as
follows:—

	£	s.	d.
In 1870	1	13	10¼
In 1876	2	12	7¾
In 1877	2	17	11

The *increase* in the value of the food imports of 1876 over that of 1870 amounts to 34,247,835*l*. And this increase corresponds to an increase in the population of 1,888,000. In other words: in order to maintain this additional population, a sum of 18*l*. 2*s*. 9½*d*. per head had to be expended for the necessaries of life, comprised under the above five headings, brought from foreign countries. This seems a remarkably large sum to be expended per individual on the above-mentioned articles of food, and it would seem as though this large increase in the imports were more than sufficient for the increase in population, and that the increase in importation must be augmented by an accompanying decrease in home production. On examining the agricultural statistics for 1870 and 1876 more closely this will be found to be the case. The following table shows the acreage under the various crops for the years 1870 and 1876 respectively, and the acreage per head of population for each year [1]:—

[1] The acreage per head of the population for the year 1891 is as follows (population, 37,880,000):—

Acres under	1870		1876	
	Acres	Acres per head of Population	Acres	Acres per head of Population
Wheat	3,773,663	0·120	3,125,342	0·094
Barley	2,623,752	0·084	2,762,263	0·083
Oats	4,424,586	0·141	4,298,722	0·129
Rye	74,527	0·002	64,951	0·019
Beans	539,968	0·017	528,556	0·016
Peas	318,607	0·010	295,012	0·008
Total	11,755,053	0·376	11,074,846	0·334

Thus the total acreage under grain crops (including beans and peas) shows a decrease of 680,207 acres in 1876 as compared with 1870. For each particular crop, except one (barley), there is less acreage in 1876 than there was in 1870, and for each particular crop, without exception, there is less acreage per head of the population in 1876 than in 1870. The decrease in the total acreage amounts to 0·042 acre per head of the popu-

	Acres	Acres per head of Population
Wheat	2,388,661	0·063
Barley	2,291,097	0·060
Oats	4,113,604	0·108
Rye	60,070	0·001
Beans	358,844	0·009
Peas	204,866	0·005
	9,417,142	0·248

The reduction in acreage under the above crops is very striking (G. C. C.).

lation. In 1877 the acreage under the above crops amounted to 11,103,196, being an increase of 28,350 acres over 1876 ; but owing to the increase in the population the acreage per head of the population was only 0·332 acre, being a decrease of 0·002 acre per head as compared with 1876.

On going back a few years we find that the falling off in the acreage is still more remarkable than that above quoted, showing that the food products of England are steadily decreasing, not only relatively to the population, but absolutely. It is impossible to get thoroughly accurate figures on this subject, but the following for 1841 are taken from the 'Encyclopædia Britannica,' printed in 1842, and are no doubt approximately correct. The figures are for *England* and *Wales* only.

Acres under	1841		1876	
	Acres	Acres per head of Population	Acres	Acres per head of Population
Wheat . .	3,800,000	0·236	2,917,765	0·120
Barley and rye	900,000	0·056	2,310,004	0·095
Oats and beans	3,000,000	0·187	2,267,892	0·093
Total . .	7,700,000	0·480	7,495,661	0·308
Population .	16,035,198		24,244,010	

Thus, in the thirty-five years from 1841 to

1876 the total acreage under wheat, barley, rye, oats, and beans has *decreased* by 204,339 acres, while the population has increased from 16,035,198 to 24,244,010. The acreage per head of the population has decreased from 0·480 acre per head in 1841 to 0·308 acre in 1876; a decrease of 0·172 acre per head. It is very remarkable to note that the acreage under wheat per head of the population in 1876 is almost exactly half of what it was in 1841; being 0·120 acre in 1876 against 0·236 acre in 1841.

These statistics are, we think, sufficient to convince the most sceptical that England is dependent to a very large extent on foreign countries for the necessaries of life. England seems to have reached the limit of her food-producing capacity some years ago, since which time any increase to her population must be maintained entirely by foreign-grown food. Judging from the foregoing statistics, it is probable that at the present time fully one-third of the population is thus maintained, and more than one-half is dependent on foreign-grown wheat for bread.

Under such a condition of things it would be extremely interesting and valuable to know what the surplus population of the United Kingdom numbers —that is, the number of those persons who could be spared from the population, without impairing the 'national efficiency'—those whose labour is not required in the United Kingdom, and which, if transferred to another part of the Empire, would be more productive, and the wealth of the nation thus largely increased. For it must be apparent that is a completely false system of economy which, by charitable donations and otherwise, gives large sums of money for the purpose of importing food to maintain in idleness and semi-idleness large numbers of people who, if transferred to other parts of the Empire, would be not only self-supporting, but (under a federal system) largely contributory to the national wealth. Unfortunately, however, there are no statistics that will give information on this subject. Though, doubtless, the number of such persons is very large, it can only be arrived at by conjecture. The statistics of pauperism will help towards forming an estimate of the number. The numbers of paupers (exclusive of vagrants) for the United Kingdom for the years 1870 and 1876, together with their cost of maintenance, are as follows[1]:—

[1] The number of paupers in the United Kingdom for the year 1893 was 1,029,405, and their cost, approximately, 12,250,000*l.*; this is a large increase in cost over the following figures, the reason for which is not apparent (G. C. C.).

	Number	Cost
		£
1870	1,279,499	9,363,797
1876	932,283	9,135,058
Decrease	347,216	228,739

The numbers show a marked diminution, though the cost of maintenance does not diminish proportionately, and the sum expended still amounts to the very respectable figure of 9,135,058*l.*, or 5*s.* 6*d.* per head of the gross population. This sum, however, is but a portion of the immense amount which is annually expended in England in private and public charities, in helping to maintain large numbers of the people in semi-idleness. How large this number may be it is impossible to say accurately, but where we have a million paupers supported absolutely by taxes levied on the people, we may, we think, safely conclude that there are at least twice as many more who are half supported by begging and charity, and who are valueless to the nation as workers, their labour being insufficient to support themselves, and only having the practical effect of taking away work from another equal number of people who would otherwise be fully employed.

IMPERIAL FEDERATION

These three million people cost the United Kingdom for their support on the above supposition an annual sum of 18,000,000*l.*, which, capitalised at four per cent., represents a capital sum of 450,000,000*l.* If these people were transferred from the United Kingdom, where their labour is not required, to some other part of the Empire where they would be self-supporting, and not only self-supporting, but also producers, clearly the above annual outlay would be saved, and the national wealth increased by a capital sum equal to 450,000,000*l.* But there would not only be this saving effected, there would also be the direct gain on account of these people becoming producers. The money value of an immigrant to the nation whither he goes, when that nation has useful work for him to do, is, as we have already said, ordinarily assumed in the United States at 1,000 dollars, or 200*l.* per head. The transfer of these people would therefore represent a direct increase to the national wealth of 600,000,000*l.*, which, combined with the saving effected, would represent a total increase of 1,050,000,000*l.*

All this, however, presupposes that the emigrant in leaving the United Kingdom and going to one of the Colonies does not become lost to the British nation—does not become less a subject of England than if he had continued to live in England—presupposes, in fact, that there is established throughout the Empire a federal system, that would accord to each district, and to every subject, no matter in what part of the Empire he resided, similar political rights, privileges, and responsibilities.

Let us now consider a few figures in regard to the size and development of the great Colonial dependencies of Great Britain. Many of the figures are taken from a lecture delivered by the Right Hon. W. E. Forster on 'Our Colonial Empire,' in Edinburgh, in 1875. First as to extent—

	Square Miles
Australia and New Zealand, about	3,100,000
South Africa	225,000
North America	3,350,000
Total	6,675,000

While the extent of all Europe is only 3,787,469 square miles. The above estimate also takes no note of the tropical possessions and the numerous smaller dependencies.

The population for 1871 is given by Mr. Forster as follows [1]:—

[1] The population at the present time is as follows:—

Australia and New Zealand	4,000,000
South Africa	2,000,000
North America (Canada and Newfoundland)	5,000,000
	11,000,000

Australia and New Zealand, about . .	2,000,000
South Africa	850,000
North America	3,750,000
Total	6,600,000

It is, however, when we consider the growth of the population, as Mr. Forster points out, that we are impressed with the wonderful strength and vitality of the Colonies. Thus, in 1850 the population recorded for the Colonies under consideration was :—

Australia and New Zealand, about . .	550,000
South Africa	400,000
North America	2,500.000
Total	3,450,000

showing an increase in twenty-one years at the rate of 91 per cent. Well may he ask, ' What will be the future increase ? '

On examining the agricultural statistics of the Colonies combined with the statistics of population, we cannot fail to be impressed with the wonderful development that is taking place. Take those of Canada for the years

Though the increase in population in these Colonies has been satisfactory, it must be confessed that it has not been as rapid as seemed probable twenty years ago. The great fall in the value of agricultural products that has taken place of late years (brought about by various complex causes) has had the effect of lowering the inducement to adopt an agricultural life in the Colonies, and has checked the inflow of population. Doubtless, too, the adoption of high protective tariffs in most of the Colonies has had a similar effect.

1841 and 1871. The statistics are not so full or complete as those that can be obtained for Great Britain; still, such as they are, they serve for purposes of comparison. In the following table the 'acres under culture' represent land that has been actually broken up and reclaimed from the wilderness :—

	1841		1871	
	Population	Acres under Culture	Population	Acres under Culture
Ontario.	455,688	1,811,431	1,620,851	8,833,626
Quebec.	697,084	2,671,768	1,191,516	5,703,944
Nova Scotia.	202,575	¹ 600,000	387,800	1,627,091
New Brunswick.	156,162	435,861	285,594	1,171,157
Manitoba	4,704	4,041	12,228	¹ 18,000
P. E. Island.	47,042	¹ 178,041	94,021	445,103
British Columbia.	—	—	10,586	¹ 12,000
	1,563,255	5,701,142	3,602,596	17,810,921
Acreage per head of Population		3·646 acres		4·944 acres

For the same years the corresponding statistics for England and Wales are as follows :—

	1841	1871
Acreage under culture (including permanent pasture).	28,749,000	29,709,249
Population	16,035,198	24,244,010
Acreage per head	1·792	1·221

¹ Estimated.

Thus, while in England in 1841 the acreage under culture amounted to $1\frac{3}{4}$ acre per head of the population, in Canada it amounted to $3\frac{1}{2}$ acres; and in England in 1871, while the acreage had *decreased* to $1\frac{1}{4}$ acre per head, in Canada it had increased to 5 acres per head. And during these thirty years, while the population of England had increased 51 per cent., in Canada it had increased 130 per cent. Perhaps no other facts could be adduced which show more clearly and concisely England's growing dependence on foreign countries for food supplies, and at the same time Canada's growing capability for furnishing these supplies.[1]

These statistics refer only to what has been done in Canada, and do not exhibit the enormous undeveloped resources which only require labour to be converted into wealth. The wheat lands of the great North-West alone, comprising Manitoba and the Saskatchewan country, are given by perfectly trustworthy authorities at over 250,000 square miles in extent—160,000,000 acres!—more than five times the whole cultivated area of England

---

[1] Canadian statistics have been used in making the above comparison; but similar statistics hold good for all the large dependencies of the Empire.

and Wales. And this, be it remembered, is but a small portion of the great heritage of the British people that is lying unowned and unoccupied. One such fact as this is alone sufficient for the argument, and it would only weary the reader to adduce more figures, besides, by their very largeness, producing a feeling of vagueness and distrust.

I think it will be admitted that the foregoing statistics show conclusively that fully one-third of the population of the United Kingdom is now dependent on foreign-grown food; that the limit of the food-producing capacity of England has already been reached, and the food-bearing acreage is now stationary and perhaps decreasing; that any additional population must be supported entirely by foreign-grown food; that there is a large surplus population, valueless as workers, so maintained at a heavy expense; that the drain of emigration represents an immense sum of money annually presented by England to a foreign Power. These statistics also show that the population of the Colonies is increasing at a marvellous rate; that in Canada the increase per cent. is more than $2\frac{1}{2}$ times greater than the increase in England; that, notwithstanding this, the increase in the food-

IMPERIAL FEDERATION 55

bearing acreage of Canada is still greater than the increase in the population; that Canada alone is capable of supplying more than all the food required in the United Kingdom, and that all that is required to do this is the population to develop the immense latent resources.

To put the matter concisely: In Great Britain there is a large surplus population with an immense demand for foreign-grown food; in the Colonies there is a large undeveloped food-producing area, with an immense demand for foreign labour. How can these conditions be combined so as to be mutually satisfying?

Under a federal system, when all parts of the Empire would be tributary to, and represented in, one Imperial centre, it would be the first and most important care of the Imperial governing body to see that the resources of every part of the Empire were developed to their proper and natural extent, and that no part was left unoccupied and unproductive while another part was burdened with a heavy surplus population. This would immediately necessitate a close supervision over emigration from one part to another. In England, where the population is dense, it would be a primary object to reduce the population to the minimum required for the necessities of that part of the Empire, by encouraging in every way possible the emigration of the surplus number to those parts of the Empire where population was sparse, and where much valuable work could be done in developing the latent resources of the country. The immediate effect of this would be of high value. In the first place, the burden of supporting a large number of people in idleness or semi-idleness would be at once removed. Secondly, the wealth of that part of the Empire to which these people went would be largely increased, from the fact of their labour being employed in developing latent resources. Thirdly, this again would have a reflex action upon England, from the fact of these emigrants in their new position of ease and independence becoming large consumers of manufactured articles, thus giving a ready market for the manufactures of England and affording remunerative employment to many of their countrymen at home; while, at the same time, the produce of the agricultural labour of these emigrants would supply the needed food in England, the interchange of the commodities establishing a traffic that would find employment for many men and much capital. Fourthly, the general wealth of the Empire would thus be largely increased. Fifthly, what may be called the taxable fund at the command of the Empire would be increased by the fact of these emigrants being converted from burdens upon the general population, to being themselves wealthy and burden-bearing citizens.

It must not be imagined that what is recommended is the wholesale shipping away of confirmed paupers; such a scheme as this would without doubt fail and end disastrously; but what is aimed at is the assistance in money and otherwise of able and competent citizens to move from one part of the Empire to another, where their labour would be fully employed. Their departure would relieve the pressure of population in England; would leave room for the full and complete employment of many who are at present only partially employed, and would allow of the gradual absorption of the great army of paupers that is at present dragged at the tail of the vast social vehicle.

For the purpose of giving this assistance it would be necessary to expend a certain amount of money annually. In commercial language it would 'pay' the Empire to expend money in this manner, because the sum expended in assisting a portion of the surplus population to move from England to a part of the Empire where their labour would be of high value, would be more than recouped by the large increase that would be made to the 'taxable fund' at the command of the Empire on account of these emigrants becoming independent and productive citizens, instead of, as formerly, being themselves burdens on the community.

After a few years of such assistance as this the surplus population of England would have been gradually and quietly transferred to another part of the Empire, while during the same time the pauper population would have been gradually dying off or absorbed into the community again. When the pressure of population had once been adjusted by these artificial means, it would of itself maintain a true balance by the action of the laws of supply and demand.

Without some such system of assisted emigration as that above indicated it is impossible for the true surplus population—those for whom there is no work, or only partial employment—ever to leave the country. For, by the very fact of their being unemployed, or only partially employed, it is impossible for them to raise the necessary capital, small though this may be, to make a start. Under the present system of leaving emigration to take care of itself those who emigrate are the industrious, energetic, far-seeing members of the labouring community—those who, ambitious of a greater success than is likely to be obtained in England from their hard-earned wages, by abstinence and self-denial, contrive to save sufficient money to start them in the new country. They are not of the 'surplus population'—they are the flower of the labouring classes of the community, men of energy, pluck, and determination above the average of their fellows, and who evince their superiority by boldly striking out for themselves a new line. When England has annually for the last half century poured thousands of such men into the United States, can we wonder at the amazing strides that country has made in manufactures, arts, and sciences, at the extraordinary energy and activity of her people, or at the very high average of intellectual vigour that obtains among her labouring class? Rather should we wonder were it otherwise.

To this it may be objected that the United

States and the Colonial dependencies of the Empire have stood in the same position relatively to England in regard to emigration, that England has neither encouraged nor obstructed emigration to either the one or the other, that therefore the Colonies had as good a chance to obtain 'the flower of the labouring classes' as had the States; and if they have not obtained a proportionate share of this emigrant population it must be owing to the inferiority of the Colonies as places of settlement. This, however, is an erroneous view. The true cause of the great flow of emigration to the United States lies in the fact that for a hundred years the United States has been a compact and energetic nation (or, until lately, twin nations), whose great object has been to attract emigrants to her shores. As population is, of course, the backbone of any country, so no money was grudged, and no labour withheld if the result attained was the addition of permanent settlers in the country. Means often the reverse of honest, agents frequently the most unscrupulous, were employed to induce emigrants to shape their course to her land: once in the country it was an easy matter to find employment to keep them there. Against

such a force as this what could a few scattered
and disconnected provinces do in the battle
for emigrants? It is only within a comparatively few years that the Canadian provinces
have enjoyed 'responsible government'—that
is, government by the election of popular representatives. It is only since the establishment of this form of government that the
various provinces have been in a position to
offer inducements to emigrants—have been in
a position to enter the lists with the United
States in the struggle for the much-coveted
labourer. And even then, what could a few
weak and poor provinces do separately and
single-handed against the united strength,
wealth, and energy of the States? Clearly,
any one of these provinces was incompetent
to deal with the great question of the internal
settlement of the country—the larger matters
of emigration—involving as this settlement
does the opening up of the country by the
construction of canals, roads, and railways.
And when we reflect that it is barely ten years
since these separate provinces were united
under one central parliament; that for barely
ten years have they known the strength that
comes of union; that it is less than ten years
since the great wheat lands of the North-West

have been placed under such control as to allow of their being settled at all—we must own that Canada has had to fight a most uneven battle with the States in the struggle to obtain emigrants. Indeed, had the diplomatists of England desired to form a great and powerful nation out of the United States, they could have hit upon no surer expedient for doing so than that of splitting up all the neighbouring British territory into small provinces, each with its independent governmental centre, while the emigration from England was left to itself—to flow to the country that could send out the most energetic emigration agents, and afford to spend the most money in attracting emigration to its shores.

But how different would the tale be had England thrown all her wealth and energy in the scale against the United States, had she, instead of looking on in an indifferent manner as though it were no concern of hers, used all her endeavour to induce her surplus population to move to her own territory, had spent her money for the purpose of opening up the treasures of her distant possessions? There can be little doubt but that the greater number of those who left her shores would have remained in the Empire, and the population of the Colonies might to-day have numbered its tens of millions.[1]

It is useless, however, to cry over 'what might have been' unless to deduce therefrom lessons for the future.

Emigration from England will go on in the future as in the past. If it is left unheeded as heretofore the greater number of emigrants will go to the United States, and, as formerly, they will be the flower of the labouring class. But if England exercises a wise control over emigration, if she exerts herself to induce her surplus population to emigrate to her own territory, if she gives her money to open up the vast resources of her possessions, the stream of emigration will rapidly be diverted to the fertilising of her own land. She will then find herself possessed of lands capable of supplying tenfold all the food that is required for the support of her people at home. She will find rapidly growing a population that in the near future will outnumber what

[1] The population of the American Colonies (now included in the United States), at the accession of George III. (1760), is given in Greene's *History of the English People* at about 1,500,000. It now numbers (1879) close on 45,000,000, an increase of thirty times in a little over 100 years, while in the same period the population of England and Wales has increased barely four times.

the most sanguine dreamer may even have foretold; she will find at her feet wealth more stupendous than any nation has ever known.

But for the fulfilment of this there must be established a federation of the Empire by which the whole Empire would be held together under one governmental control. Under no other system could England be recouped for the outlay made in developing the Colonies. Under the present system, as pointed out before, every pound that England spends on her Colonies, every man she sends thither, only hastens the day when her Colonies will be independent nations. It is natural, therefore, that she should refuse to spend any money on their development or grudgingly allow her people to emigrate thither.

The question of emigration has been dwelt upon thus fully, because it is apparent that upon it hangs the question of the Federation of the Empire. The matter placed in brief stands as follows:—Every year a large number of people must leave the United Kingdom in order to find room to live in other parts of the world. Shall England control this emigration and direct it to her Colonies, or shall she pay no heed to it? If she pays no heed to it, then annually the flower of her population will be drained away to enrich a foreign Power or to build up new nations in the Colonial possessions of England. And at no very distant day, perhaps, England will find herself circumscribed to the narrow limits of the United Kingdom, weighted with the burden of a large pauper population, forced to pay immense sums annually to foreign countries for food, while possibly at the same time her manufactures are excluded from all countries by inimical tariff regulations, or by the development of manufactures in other places. On the other hand, if England controls this emigration, if she expends large sums of money in developing her Colonial possessions, in transporting her surplus population to these outlying parts of the Empire, how is she to be reimbursed for this outlay? how is she to benefit by the increased wealth of these outlying parts unless she is empowered to collect revenue from them? And, again, how can she collect revenue from these places unless she accords to them a proportionate voice in the government of the Empire—in other words, unless there is established a federation of the Empire?

From a purely Colonial point of view a

federation of the Empire would also be of great benefit. Though the Colonies are not like the Mother Country dependent on other places for food, though they have within themselves undeveloped resources which will ultimately afford all the manufactured articles they may require—though by slow accretions and natural growth their population will reach immense proportions—yet their progress will be much slower than if assisted by the energy and wealth of the Mother Country. In the case of Canada alone the immense outlay of money required to open up the resources of the North-West by the construction of the Pacific Railway will be a burden almost too great for the present comparatively small population to bear, while if this work were largely assisted by the Imperial Government, as no doubt in the event of a federation of the Empire it would be, the burden would be but lightly felt, while the increase in the general wealth of the nation by the settlement of this valuable country would more than balance the outlay.

No doubt, in the event of a federation of the Empire being adopted, there are many difficult and delicate matters which would require very skilful handling for their proper

adjustment. Prominent among these we may mention :—
 1. Apportioning of the National Debt.
 2. Adjustment of taxation.
 3. Mode of raising the revenue.

It is to be presumed that all duties between various parts of the Empire would be abolished, and as each part could supply what the other lacked there would be less necessity to import from foreign countries, and the revenue derived from custom dues would consequently be much diminished. These and kindred matters, though not insurmountable obstacles, yet offer great difficulties, and open up questions large enough and interesting enough to require separate treatment.

I have already pointed out that the development of the Colonies under the present Colonial system can result only in the establishment of independent and separate nations, and how necessary it is for the material well-being of England as a nation that these outlying parts of the Empire should be retained. I have also shown how the retaining of these outlying parts can only be effected by the adoption of a federation of the Empire; and the question which daily becomes more vital is whether this vast agglomeration of loosely-connected States shall be moulded by some master hand into one grand, stupendous Empire, unparalleled in its extent, unequalled in its wealth, and unrivalled in its political institutions, or allowed slowly to melt away and break up into numerous third-rate Powers.

CHAPTER III

WE have now to consider the practical working of an Imperial federal system. It will, perhaps, be best to deal first with the question of representation.

As briefly stated before, the governing principles in carrying out a federation of the Empire are the separation of Imperial from local affairs in parliamentary government, and the representation by popular election of all parts of the Empire in the Imperial Parliament.

These are the main principles as broadly stated, though they are subject to limitations. Thus, in the matter of representation, it would not be either desirable or necessary that *every* Colonial possession should be directly represented, as many of the very small Colonies would not be of sufficient importance to be accorded representation in the Imperial House; but as each Colony grew and developed it would ultimately be accorded this representation. The precise stage in the life of a Colony at which it would arrive at this representation would be a matter to be decided as circumstances required. That is to say, it would not be advisable to create any definite and fixed standard—based either upon population, wealth, or extent—by which to regulate the admission to the Imperial Parliament, and to grant this admission only when that standard had been attained. No doubt the population, wealth, and extent would always form the chief and important elements in the question of admission to the Imperial House; still it would be injudicious to assign any definite quantitative value to these elements, as this value might, and probably would, vary with different Colonies. The main point, however, to be insisted upon is the adoption of the principle that ultimately each Colony should arrive at this representation, and that the fully-developed state in the political life of each Colony is that of being merged in the political life of the Empire at large. Every step should be taken with this final goal in view.

It will no doubt be objected to this, as has already been objected by Lord Blachford, that the interests of the various Colonies are so diverse, that the physical conditions of each are so different, as to render any community of interest, such as would be necessary for the working of an Imperial House, impossible of being attained. To this it may be answered that, in spite of these apparent diversities and differences, this community of interest *does* exist, and exists even now, in spite of the want of any central point in which these interests may be focussed and practically utilised. There would be at least this one grand purpose, which would be common to every part of the Empire—the maintenance of the Empire. There is undoubtedly throughout the Colonies a strong love for the Mother Country, a strong desire to remain connected with the Mother Country, and evidence of the practical outcome from these feelings is afforded in the offers of military assistance which have been tendered to England by the Colonies, when the Colonies have nothing to gain and everything to lose by such assistance. Would not these feelings be immensely strengthened by having a definite object afforded to them in the maintenance of one compact Empire under a supreme parliamentary chamber? The argument drawn from the physical and geographical view of the case is captious and unsound. As well might it be said that the people of the Orkney Islands have no interests in common with the people of the West of Ireland, and that, therefore, it would be unwise to form a parliamentary chamber affording representation to such disconnected places. And no doubt two hundred years ago, and even less, this would have been true; no such community of feeling could have existed between the Orkney Islands and the West of Ireland as to have rendered representation in one parliament at Westminster, under any circumstances, possible; the separation, geographically and intellectually, was too complete. But just as during the last two hundred years the increase of population, the extension of knowledge, the development of means of communication, the integration and differentiation of the people of the United Kingdom, have rendered this representation not only possible but imperatively necessary; so the same causes at work throughout the whole Empire during more recent years have now resulted in a similar effect. The Empire of the future, if maintained at all, must be maintained under a system of parliamentary representation of all parts of the Empire. If sectional feelings are to have weight, then the arguments adduced against affording representation in the Imperial Parliament to the Colonies might be adduced with equal force as between England, Scotland, and Ireland. The argument drawn from the geographical separation is of little force. As a writer in the 'Westminster Review'[1] says on this subject: 'As to the geographical argument, it is each year becoming more obsolete; we laugh at distance! Australia is not so far off now as John o' Groat's was a century ago. Swift steamers and ocean cables make Melbourne as near to us as Dublin. It is too late, when we can transmit men by steam and messages by electricity, to urge that distance is a bar to government.' And each year this bar that once existed becomes less and less; until, by the perfection of the means of travelling and communication, it will be as little personal inconvenience to a man of business to represent a constituency at Westminster as at Ottawa.

Another matter on which there would be a strong community of interest would be emigration. Under a federal system it would be the duty and care of the Imperial Govern-

[1] 'Our Colonial Empire,' *Westminster Review,* April 1876.

ment to see that emigration from the Mother Country to those parts of the Empire where there were great latent resources to be developed was properly stimulated and encouraged. It would be necessary to spend considerable sums of money every year in assisting emigrants to go out to Canada, Australia, or the Cape. The effect of this would be to reduce the pressure in the labour market at home, while those who went away would be placed in positions of comparative ease and comfort. It has been shown in a previous chapter that it is only under the federal system that Government assistance can be given to emigrants; and that it is only under a system of assistance that the poorer classes—the true surplus—can ever afford to emigrate. It was shown also that under the federal system not only did it become possible to give this assistance, but that it became a prime duty to afford it, and that it would be an extremely self-injurious policy on the part of the nation to refuse it. See, then, the result to which we are driven. Federation of the Empire means, for the unemployed and the poor, assisted passages to various parts of the Empire, where their labour would command a remunerative price. It means transplanting them from squalor, destitution, and misery, to comparative ease, plenty, and comfort. To the Colonies, on the other hand, federation of the Empire would mean a plentiful supply of labourers; it would mean a rapid and complete opening up and peopling of the country; an amazing renewing of the national vigour. From a purely national standpoint this would seem to imply sufficient community of interests to make a federation workable. But what shall we say when we consider the individual interests of those benefited by this national emigration? Take the case of a labouring man in England. Even by the utmost prudence and economy it is impossible for him to support himself and his family, and at the same time lay by any money worth the naming to guard against less prosperous times. When dull times come, as they do periodically, his little savings are swallowed up in a few weeks, or, at most, months. He has to rely on charity and poor-rates for subsistence, while his misery is increased tenfold, and a fresh bitterness added to his degradation by the sight of his starving little ones. Tell such a man (and there are thousands such in England at the present day) of a land beyond the seas where he can get plenty of work, where he can place his family beyond the horrors of starvation; tell him that the Government will pay his passage out to this new country, will assist him to start in the new life, and would not his heart bound with new hope, would not his whole being be moved to new action? If the working men of England, the unemployed of the Mother Country, understood the federation of the Empire in this sense, every other political question would sink into insignificance before it. Federation of the Empire would be *the* question of the day. It would be discussed in every working-man's club; it would be advocated at every meeting; it would be made the test question at every polling-booth. For the philanthropist there could be no work the consummation of which would confer such immeasurable benefits on his fellow-men as the federation of the Empire. Not only for the present would the condition of the poor be immensely improved, but for an indefinitely long time their descendants would be placed in positions where, by their own industry and perseverance, they could live in comfort and plenty.

Again, on viewing the trade aspect of the case, we shall discover a sufficient community of interest to render a federation of the Empire desirable. Within the last fifty years the wonderful development of the means of communication has almost revolutionised the older systems of trading. Raw material from remote corners of the earth is poured into England, there to be worked into useful articles, and again exported in its finished state to far distant countries. Distance is no bar to trade. The flannel shirt worn by the Canadian farmer, and which he has bought at the little country 'store,' is probably made from wool clipped from an Australian sheep, has been manufactured in some English factory, and again carried some thousands of miles by sea and rail before it reaches its final purchaser. And all this has been done at a less cost, and a better garment is obtained, than if the farmer had clipped the wool from one of his own flock. The cost of carrying the material this immense distance is probably less than was the cost in former times of conveying it from London to Birmingham. Again, the cheese made on the Canadian farm is perhaps purchased on account of its superiority and cheapness by some London artisan. To a far greater extent than ever before is England now dependent upon countries outside of herself for the prime necessaries of her physical and commercial existence.[1] Like a great tree, her roots have struck into far distant countries, while her branches overshadow the most remote lands. As it is impossible for the English people to live unless supplied with food from other countries, so it is impossible for English trade to live unless it has access to other countries. Recognising this, it may be asked, What precautions has England taken, what political safeguards has she adopted, in order to secure and maintain her Colonial trade? It is with amazement that I have to answer, 'None at all.' While she has spent millions of money, and poured out her blood in opening up the markets of the world, in acquiring and peopling vast possessions, in forming new markets for herself, in her Colonies she has adopted a policy towards these Colonies which puts it in the power of Colonial politicians, in order to gratify some personal ambition, or gain some party triumph, to adopt a fiscal policy that excludes English manufacturers, that shuts out English trade. No sooner is a Colony sufficiently developed to become of value to England as a purchaser of English

[1] In the last forty years the value of the export trade in English manufactured goods has increased about four times.

manufactures, than England lets slip from her hands the power that could direct or control the movements of English trade.[1] In the preceding chapter I discussed the question of Free Trade and Protection, and only need now to point out to the British manufacturer and the British taxpayer how the volume and direction of British trade is immediately and directly affected by the fiscal policy adopted by the various British Colonies. Under a system of 'protection,' with the object of fostering Colonial manufactures, British trade is injured and British merchants suffer. In order to maintain a fiscal system throughout the Empire that would insure the Colonial markets for British manufactures, it is apparent that the fiscal policy of the Empire must be under the control of the Empire—that is, of one chief parliamentary chamber of the Empire; and this implies federation. Under the present Colonial system it is impossible for England to exert any restraint over the fiscal policy of her Colonies; if they choose to adopt Protection, England cannot choose but agree to it. But it must be apparent to every British manufacturer upon rightly viewing the trade

[1] This not in the Protectionist sense, but in the sense of preventing inimical legislation.

question, that there is sufficient community of interest between himself and his fellow-subjects in the Colonies to render a federation of the Empire desirable.

Granting, then, that this parliamentary representation is a necessary element in the maintenance of the unity of the Empire, let us now inquire how this representation may be best effected. To this question there seems to be but one answer. The representation must be effected by the election of members to serve in the Imperial House. All parts of the Empire (that are fully admitted to the federation) must be represented in a similar manner. It has been proposed, however, by Sir Julius Vogel and others, that a Council should be formed of Colonial representatives, which should officially advise the Colonial Secretary or the House of Commons on Colonial matters, and that the representation of the Colonies should be effected in this manner. This might, perhaps, be a judicious manner in which gradually to introduce the federal system, but it is impossible that this could be the ultimate and final form that the Colonial representation would assume. If the federation of the Empire is an accomplished fact, why should Canada or Australia be represented in a more imperfect manner in the Imperial House than is Scotland? Is it reasonable to suppose that as Canada or Australia grow in wealth and population they would be satisfied to be represented in the Imperial Chamber only in a second-hand manner? If the Empire is one, all parts should have equal rights, and all parts should have a proportionate share in the governing of the Empire. Representation by a Council, as proposed, would be simply a continuance of the present system; it would not afford representation in the Imperial House to all parts of the Empire.

The objection that seems to be always supreme in the minds of most Englishmen in dealing with this question of Colonial representation in the Imperial House is that already the House of Commons is too large and unwieldy to do its work, and that to admit Colonial members and bring in Colonial questions to the House would so increase the business and enlarge the talking capacity of the House as to bring all business to a standstill. Already it is found impossible to get through the business of a session during the sittings of the House, and every year numerous measures are shelved without, from lack of time, having been considered at all; while upon some popular question the time of the House is utterly wasted in listening to the repetition *ad nauseam* of the same ideas and opinions by members who feel it to be their duty to make speeches in order to have them read by their constituents. So pronounced has this evil become of late, and so great are the difficulties of carrying through the necessary business of the House, that we have at the conclusion of every session a long list of bills that have been thrown aside from sheer inability of the House to take up their consideration, while the press teems with suggestions for the expediting of public business. From an article published in the 'Times' of May 6, 1878, it appears that the total number of measures before the House during the then current session was 147 public bills and 275 private bills. How many of the 147 bills became law at the termination of the session might be hard to say, but after three months' work only fifteen had been consummated, while four others had gone up to the House of Lords, and of the remainder only thirty-nine passed a second reading. Of the 275 private bills, besides those of a purely personal nature, there were ninety-six railway bills, thirty-one tramway bills, thirty-one water bills, twenty-four gas bills, eighteen docks and harbours bills, and forty-nine local improvements bills. These private bills would appear, all of them, to be of a purely local nature, and not such as should require the deliberations of the highest chamber of the Empire. As the writer of the article says : 'Why the Imperial Legislature should have to ratify arrangements for empowering a landlord to grant leases for ninety-nine years instead of twenty-one when he and all persons interested in the property have already decided the change to be for their common benefit, it might be hard to explain to a German or French deputy.' No doubt it would, and the same might be said of most, if not all, of the private bills. Again, the same article says : 'The conclusion is obvious, and has been recognised for years past, that Parliament undertakes more work than it can ever accomplish.' Here in these two sentences there is a recognition of the fact that Parliament is not only overburdened with work, but also undertakes work that is somewhat derogatory to the high functions of an Imperial Chamber.

To cure these defects in the parliamentary system in a thorough and complete manner, there would seem to be but one course to be adopted—viz., to separate the local from the

Imperial measures, and, by forming a Local House of Parliament for the consideration of the former, thus leave the Imperial House so much the more untrammelled to deal with Imperial matters. The gain to parliamentary legislation by this course would be immediate and direct. The Local House would be of manageable and compact proportions; its members would be able to devote their time and energies to the proper treatment and consideration of various local questions; the dissatisfaction caused at present throughout the country by the constant burking of local measures would be allayed; and we might even hope that the Irish difficulty would be set at rest, perhaps by the formation of an Irish Local Parliament, but in any case by reason of the House being able to devote proper time and attention to the consideration of Irish grievances. In a similar manner, the Imperial House would be much reduced in bulk and proportionately increased in activity and vitality. Its time would be occupied in the consideration of Imperial questions; its energy would not then be frittered away upon petty local matters; nor would the business of the House be obstructed by members anxious to force the consideration of some local grievance.

Such a rearrangement of the parliamentary system would expedite public business to a degree that could not be attained by any other system; and, considering the constant and steady growth of parliamentary business, it would seem that recourse must be had to some such system in order to carry on the ordinary business of the country. Nor would this rearrangement require that any violence should be done to the English parliamentary system; it would not introduce any new principle, such as would be the case if a large part of the Empire were to be represented by an Advisory Board, as has been suggested; it would simply be to adopt the confederation system that has been found to work so smoothly in Germany and the United States. A scheme of this nature to facilitate the despatch of parliamentary business was put forward some years ago by Earl Russell, and the fact that so experienced a parliamentarian as he favoured the idea is somewhat of a guarantee that it is not impracticable.

But it will at once be seen how easily and naturally, by the adoption of this system, the representation of the Colonies would be effected. There would no longer be any objection to the admission of Colonial representatives to the

Imperial House; the matters submitted to the House would be matters of Imperial interest, matters upon which representatives of any or every part of the Empire would have a right to express an opinion, and upon which they would be in a position to form sound judgments or offer valuable advice. In the Imperial House every part of the Empire would, as a matter of right, be represented. The Imperial House would stand in the same relation to Australia or Canada as to England or Ireland.

I will now venture to submit a general scheme for the Imperial and Local Houses, chiefly with the hope of evoking discussion on, and developing public interest in, the subject.

The Imperial House might be composed of 300 members, distributed in the following manner:—

England	185
Scotland	25
Ireland	40 [1]
Colonies	50
	300

This would retain pretty nearly the proportions in which the members are allotted at

[1] The proportion of Irish members is now too large, in view of the decrease of Irish population and the increase of other parts of the Empire (G. C. C., 1895).

present. This, while granting the principle of Colonial representation, and admitting the representatives in a sufficient number to give proper weight to Colonial views and sentiments, would yet leave a proper preponderance of power on the side of England. Of course it is to be expected that with the growth and increase of the distant parts of the Empire, there would go an increase in the representation.

The Colonial representation might be distributed in the first instance as follows:—

Dominion of Canada and Newfoundland	20
Australia	15
New Zealand	5
Cape Settlements	5
West Indies	5
	50

These members would be chosen by popular election, and the requisite electoral districts would be marked off in the various countries.

The Ministry of the day would be drawn from members of the Imperial House and the House of Lords, and these Ministers would be the immediate and responsible advisers of her Majesty.

The sittings of the House would take place annually in London, and would be of five years' duration, unless terminated by a dissolution.

The matters falling within the province of the Imperial House to deal with would be chiefly comprised under the following heads :—

Maintenance of the Royal Family.
Control of the Army and Navy.
Relations with foreign Powers.
Inter-provincial relations with various parts of the Empire.
Marine and shipping affairs.
Customs and finance.
Postal affairs.
Justice.

These would probably represent the chief heads of business. The 'postal affairs' would probably include the entire management and control of the Post Office business throughout the United Kingdom, but throughout the various Colonies the internal management of the Post Office would, perhaps, be better left to the Local Houses. Under 'justice' would be included the establishment of Supreme Courts of Appeal in various parts of the Empire. The power to appoint judges to these Courts would be retained in the hands of the Imperial Government. Each of these Courts would be a final Court for its respective locality. The matters of customs and finance will be more fully treated of further on.

The following is a sketch of the Local House for England or Ireland :—

The country would be under a Viceroy or Governor, appointed by the Queen in Council. The advisers of the Viceroy would be drawn from the members of the Local House, and the relations of the Viceroy to his Ministers would be precisely analogous to those of the Queen to her Ministers. The size of the Local House would, perhaps, be as follows :—

	Members
England	250
Scotland	35
Ireland	65
	350

This is assuming that the United Kingdom would be represented in one Local House.

All measures passed by the Local House would require the assent of the Viceroy before they could become law. But any measure of doubtful constitutionality could be 'reserved' by the Viceroy, in which case the bill would be remitted for the consideration of the Queen in Council, and either passed or vetoed. Also any measure passed by the Local House, and assented to by the Viceroy, could be annulled if vetoed by the Queen in Council within two years from the time of assent. These provisions have been adopted in Canada as between the Governor-General and the Lieutenant-Governors, and as between the Queen and the Governor-General, so as to preserve a proper control over provincial or local legislation. Copies of all bills assented to by the Viceroy would be immediately forwarded to the Secretary of State for her Majesty's consideration.

The local Colonial Legislatures would remain much as at present. The appointment of Colonial governors would rest with the Queen in Council. With respect to Canada, where confederation has already been adopted, it would probably be found that the Dominion House could assume some of the work now performed by the Provincial Legislatures, as some of the work done by the Dominion House would be transferred to the Imperial Parliament. The effect of this would be to render possible a further concentration of the Provincial Legislatures (such as legislative union of the Maritime Provinces) with a proportionate gain in legislative wisdom. No doubt, in time, with the development and perfecting of the municipal system of governing, the ultimate result would be to do away with all the Provincial Legislatures, and leave the present Dominion House as the one Local Legislative Assembly for Canada.

In the foregoing sketch nothing has been said about a second chamber. For the local legislatures a second chamber would not be required. The veto power vested in her Majesty in Council would hold a complete check on any unconstitutional measures, and, after all, it is only against such measures as these that it is possible or even desirable to guard. Under our Constitution, which may be called a 'limited democracy,' the will of the bulk of the people must ultimately become law. In Canada, where we have an example of federation at work, each province (except Ontario) began its political life under the new *régime* with two chambers, a Legislative Assembly and a Legislative Council, corresponding to a House of Commons and a House of Lords. But each province has awoke, or is awaking, to the fact that the Upper Chamber is only an encumbrance and useless expense, and every province is following the example of Ontario in abolishing the Upper Chamber. So it would be with the Local Houses of England or Ireland. The Upper Chamber, if instituted at first, would soon be found to be unnecessary.

The House of Lords would be, as now, the Upper Chamber of the Imperial Parliament. It would be necessary to add a few life peers (perhaps twenty) to represent the Colonies. The position of the bishops in the House of Lords would undoubtedly raise a very delicate question, and a question over which much bitterness would probably be displayed. There can be no question, from a perfectly unprejudiced and dispassionate standpoint, but that the Church of England is a local matter, and that as such the bishops would no longer, *ex officio*, be entitled to a seat in the Upper Imperial Chamber.

This, then, is the scheme which is suggested for the representation of all parts of the Empire in one Imperial Chamber. Even apart from the question of a federation of the Empire, it is apparent that the parliamentary system of England would be strengthened and renewed in vigour by the formation of Local Houses and the separation of local from Imperial matters. The heterogeneous mass of legislation which the House of Commons annually attempts to digest is in marked contrast to the more carefully selected food that is supplied to the chief chambers of such countries as the United States or Germany, where the more highly-developed parliamentary system obtains. From a separation of the measures to be considered, there would result a more careful consideration of the measures, with more carefully-amended statutes. These, however, are collateral advantages; the chief result to be striven for is the formation of one great Empire—an Empire founded on so broad a base that no storms could move her; an Empire that would be mighty in war, and yet mightier in peace, whose voice would sway the councils of every nation, and whose voice would be always on the side of right, truth, and progress.

We come now to the consideration of the income and expenditure of the Empire under federation. This subject is very large and difficult, and though the scheme about to be submitted is probably far from perfect, still it will show that the plan in the main is workable, and all that is required is only more precise information and more exact knowledge in order to perfect the details.

In order to present a comprehensive view of the financial aspect of the case, there is inserted here a statement showing the condition of the various countries forming the Colonial portion of the Empire in 1875:—

	Population	Revenue	Imports	Total Trade	Debt
		£	£	£	£
Canada and Newfoundland	3,832,077	5,249,960	20,794,040	44,556,579	31,481,461
Australia and New Zealand	2,287,500	14,000,602	47,272,839	91,679,841	54,759,347
Cape and South Africa	254,073	2,506,450	6,940,157	11,983,391	2,757,058
West Indies	1,277,920	1,606,268	7,369,474	15,475,745	1,225,558
	7,651,570	23,363,280	88,376,510	163,705,559	90,223,424

While during the same year the corresponding statistics for the United Kingdom were as follows:—

	Population	Revenue	Imports	Total Trade	Debt
		£	£	£	£
United Kingdom	32,750,000	74,921,873	373,939,577	655,551,900	775,348,681

Thus, it will be seen that the Colonies comprised under the four preceding headings represent no insignificant domain either in population or trade. The value of the imports into these Colonies was greater than the value of the imports into the United States,[1] and the revenue and trade per head of the population was greater than that of the United Kingdom. The following is a tabular statement of the foregoing figures worked out upon the basis of the population:—

[1] Value of imports into United States in 1878 was 86,706,186*l*.

	Revenue	Imports	Total Trade	Debt
	£ s. d.	£ s. d.	£ s. d.	£ s. d.
Colonies, per head of Population	3 1 0½	11 11 3½	21 10 7¾	13 7 2
United Kingdom	2 5 9	11 8 4¼	20 0 4	23 19 7

Considering how rapid is the growth of the Colonies, both in population and trade, it is apparent that in comparatively few years the above items will equal those of the United Kingdom absolutely as well as relatively.

Under a federation of the Empire, the position to be aimed at is, that all the public debts of the Empire, together with other Imperial burdens, should be assumed by the Imperial Government, and that to meet this the Imperial Government should collect customs in every part of the Empire. This is the broad principle, but it would be subject to limitations. Thus, in the first instance, it would be impossible for the Imperial Government to assume the whole burden of the National Debt, without also assuming the collection of some local tax. Indeed, in order to meet four-fifths of the charges on the National Debt, it would be necessary that the Imperial Government should assume the greater part of the British excise duties as an Imperial revenue; the remaining one-fifth of the National Debt charges would have to be borne by the Local Government of England until, at any rate, the Imperial customs receipts had sufficiently increased. The collection of customs would necessarily be carried on everywhere by Imperial officers. And the fiscal policy in all parts of the Empire would be uniform, at least so far as British goods were concerned. Perhaps it would be best to introduce here a comprehensive view of this matter.

Estimated Expenditure of the Empire under Federation.

	£
Cost of National Debt, 28,411,751*l.*; four-fifths of this	22,729,400
Royal Family	550,000
Army (include Colonies and India)	17,000,000
Navy	11,000,000
Customs throughout Empire	2,000,000
Inland revenue (excise, United Kingdom)	1,000,000
Salaries of departments and expenses	2,500,000
Law and justice (include Supreme Courts of Appeal)	1,000,000
Post-office (include packet service throughout Empire)	4,000,000
Consular and foreign service	500,000
Subsidies to provinces	2,000,000
Interest on Colonial debt, 100,000,000*l.* at 3 per cent.	3,000,000
Miscellaneous, emigration, &c.	1,500,000
	£68,779,400

To balance this the receipts would be somewhat as follows:—

Estimated Revenue of the Empire under Federation.

	£
British customs—7 per cent. on 380,000,000*l*. [1]	26,600,000
Colonial customs—12 per cent. on 90,000,000*l*. [2]	10,800,000
British excise, malt . . . 7,800,000*l*. ⎫	
„ „ spirits . . 15,000,000*l*. ⎬	23,300,000
Sugar used in brewing . . 500,000*l*. ⎭	
Post-office	6,000,000
Crown lands	500,000
Suez Canal	200,000
Miscellaneous	1,500,000
Total	£68,900,000

It will be noticed that only four-fifths of the total charges on account of the National Debt are borne by the Imperial exchequer; the remaining one-fifth, amounting to 5,682,351*l*., would have to be borne by the local government of England—at least until the Imperial receipts had sufficiently grown to assume the whole burden of the debt. Probably the best plan would be for the local government to pay the above sum annually to the Imperial Government, allowing the whole management

---

[1] The value of British imports in 1875 was 373,939,577*l*.; in 1876 it was 375,154,703*l*. The amount raised by customs amounted in 1874 to 5·5 per cent., in 1875 to 5·3 per cent., and in 1876 to 5·15 per cent. on the gross value of the imports.

[2] The exact value of the imports into the Colonies for 1875 was 83,376,510*l*. The amount raised by customs in Canada in 1875 amounted to 12·48 per cent. on the gross value of the imports. In 1876 it was 12·63 per cent. The sum raised by customs in the United States in 1878 amounted to 30 per cent. upon the gross value of the imports, being 26,134,036*l*. upon a gross value of 86,706,136*l*.

of the debt to rest with the Imperial authorities. This would be the simplest way of arranging. It would be better, too, that it should be done in this way rather than that the Imperial Government should assume the collection of any other taxes—such as, for instance, the income tax. The receipts from the income tax (5,841,265*l.* for 1877–78) would more than balance this one-fifth of the National Debt charges; still it would be better that the levying of this tax should be left to the local government, and the necessary amount paid over as a subsidy to the Imperial exchequer, rather than that the Imperial Government should assume the control of so purely local a tax. With the increase of trade the increase in the Imperial receipts from customs would be sufficient to bear the whole burden of the National Debt. The increase required represents only about 50 per cent. on the Colonial trade, and this would probably be effected in a very few years,[1] and then it would not be necessary that the local government should pay the subsidy above spoken of.

[1] The value of imports into the various Colonies under consideration was about 61,500,000*l.* in 1865, as against 88,876,510*l.* in 1875, showing an increase of 43·6 per cent. in ten years. In 1890 the value of imports from all places into these various Colonies had increased only to 94,490,918*l.* Canada imported less in value in 1890 than in 1875.

The amount set down for customs throughout the Empire is for the collection of customs in all parts of the Empire. The customs officials would be appointed by the Imperial Government.

Supreme Courts of Appeal would be established in various parts of the Empire; probably one for England, one for North America, one for the West Indies, one for Australia, and one for South Africa. The judges of these Courts would be appointed by the Imperial Government. Each one of these Courts would be a final Court. The administration of justice generally would be left in the hands of the local government; these Appeal Courts being the only Courts to which the Imperial Government would appoint judges.

The item of 2,000,000*l*. for subsidies to provinces is to supplement the revenues of those provinces or Colonies where the source of revenue has been taken away by the absorption of the customs dues in an Imperial revenue. Thus, in the Dominion of Canada at the present time the Dominion Government pays subsidies to the various provinces forming the confederation amounting to a total of 801,615*l*. ($3,655,850.58 in 1876-77). These subsidies are fixed charges, and are paid in lieu of the customs receipts which these provinces resigned to the Dominion on entering confederation. But if the Dominion were to join the federation of the Empire and give up to the Imperial exchequer the customs receipts, the Imperial Government would be required to assume the burden of these provincial subsidies. As with Canada so it probably would be with some of the other Colonies, and there is, therefore, set down the sum of two millions sterling as being somewhat near the amount required to meet this expense.

The Colonial debt is placed at 100,000,000*l*. This is greater than it is at present by some six or eight millions. It would probably be advisable to allow for a substantial increase to the Colonial debt upon the eve of entering the federation.

In estimating the probable revenue the British customs receipts are calculated at 7 per cent. on the gross value of the imports. This is an increase of about $1\frac{1}{2}$ per cent. on the present rate. The additional amount raised, as compared with the present customs receipts, would be about 6,000,000*l*. On the other hand, however, there would be almost a similar remission of taxation under the local government of England (see p. 104) which would counterbalance this increase of customs. On the Colonial imports the average customs receipts are estimated at 12 per cent. *ad valorem* on the imports. This is probably less than it actually would be. As a very large proportion of the British imports (about 100,000,000*l*. out of 380,000,000*l*.) consists of staple articles of food, it would not be advisable to collect heavy duties on these, and, therefore, the British customs rate would probably average less than the Colonial on the total value of the imports, as the latter consist mainly of manufactured articles.

No doubt this question of customs is one that presents considerable difficulties; and the difficulties are much increased by the fact of some of the Colonies having adopted a system of protection. For the Imperial Government in London suddenly to revert to a revenue tariff throughout the Empire would, in protectionist countries, create great trouble, and probably dissatisfaction. In these countries it would, perhaps, be best to maintain the protectionist duties, so long as this was desired by a majority of the representatives of the particular country in the Imperial House. At the same time, however, it should be pointed out that customs dues levied between parts of the Empire are more of the nature of excise or octroi duties rather than customs duties, in an international sense; and that in these protectionist countries an octroi duty, and merely for revenue purposes, might be charged on goods entering from various parts of the Empire, while a high customs duty might be maintained in deference to the protectionist doctrines against foreign countries. This is the plan proposed by Mr. de Labilliere in his paper read before the Royal Colonial Institute, in January, 1875, and by some such compromise as this the customs difficulty might, perhaps, be overcome; but, of course, the condition ultimately to be attained is that of free trade between all parts of the Empire, while the revenue should be raised by levying customs on foreign goods. The idea has been suggested that the Imperial exchequer might be supplied by subsidies paid by the local governments, leaving the customs in the hands of the local parliaments to be dealt with. But it is not possible that this system could ever be the final and complete system under an Imperial Federation. It would be necessary that the control of the finances of the Empire should be in the hands of the Imperial Chamber, and this could not be the case if the revenue depended on subsidies from the local parliaments. In the event of an increased supply being at any time asked for for Imperial purposes, it would be competent for the local parliament to refuse it; and the granting of supplies would be seized upon by the local parliaments as an occasion to review and criticise the policy of the Imperial House, and possibly to dictate as to the future course to be pursued. Such a relation between the two Houses would be quite untenable, and would certainly ere long lead to strife and disagreement. The only perfect financial system under a federation of the Empire would be that under which the entire control of the customs and revenue was in the hands of the Imperial Parliament.

In the foregoing sketch of the financial condition of the Empire under federation, enough has been brought forward to show that the scheme is practically workable. Of course, there are many points that have only been lightly touched upon, and the working out in detail of which would require much thought and skilful handling. Still the main features have been dealt with, and the result may fairly be claimed to be satisfactory. To complete the sketch, however, and even at the risk of becoming tedious, it will be necessary to show the financial condition of the local governments under the federal system.

We will take the United Kingdom, using the statistics of the year 1877–78.

Estimated Revenue of British Local Government (Ireland included) under Federation.

	£
Stamps	11,000,000
Land and house tax	2,700,000
Income tax	5,800,000
Excise: licenses, 3,600,000*l*.; railways, 750,000*l*.	4,350,000
Telegraphs	1,350,000
Miscellaneous	2,000,000
	£27,200,000

Estimated Expenditure.

	£
One-fifth charge of National Debt	5,682,351
Courts of justice	650,000
Public works and buildings	1,500,000
Salaries and expenses of departments	1,500,000
Law and justice	5,000,000
Inland revenue	800,000
Telegraphs	1,200,000
Education, art, and science	4,000,000
Miscellaneous	1,000,000
	£21,332,351

From this it will be seen that the local revenue, as pointed out previously, shows a surplus of nearly 6,000,000*l*. over the local expenditure, and that, therefore, a reduction of taxation to this extent would be possible.

This reduction just counterbalances the increase of revenue that would be exacted by the Imperial Parliament from the increased customs duties levied on British imports. At the same time, however, it must be pointed out that, while the reduction is favourable chiefly to the richer classes of the community, the increase is obtained from all classes of the community.

To show how federation would affect the Colonial finances, we may give here the condition of Canada under the Imperial Federation. The statistics are taken from the Canadian financial Blue Book for 1876-77.

		£
Total revenue under present system		4,538,945
Less revenue transferred to Imperial Government under federation :—		
Customs £2,581,683		
Militia 2,598		2,584,281
Total Canadian revenue under federation		£1,954,664
		£
Total expenditure under present system		4,839,363
Less expenditure borne by Imperial Government under federation :—		
Debt charges . . . £1,611,826		
Militia and defence . . 119,408		
Customs 148,478		
P. O. Transatlantic Packet service 34,000		
Appeal Court . . . 10,000		
Subsidies to provinces . 752,232		2,675,944
Total Canadian expenditure under federation		£2,164,419

It will be noticed there was a deficit in the Canadian revenue amounting to 300,418*l*., and in the new scheme submitted there is still a deficit amounting to 109,755*l*. It would be necessary to provide against this deficit by a rearrangement of taxation; and as a further help towards this would be the possibility, as pointed out before, of the Dominion Government assuming duties and revenues at present performed and applied by the provincial legislatures. This would, doubtless, more than wipe out the deficit, but it is unnecessary here to go further into details on this point. The revenue and expenditure of the various other Colonies entering the federation would be treated in a similar manner.

It may be thought painful to have gone so far into this question of revenue and expenditure, while as yet there is but little (if any) practical movement in the direction of an Imperial Federation, but it is apparent that the whole scheme ultimately hangs upon this. If federation cannot be shown to be workable financially, then, no matter how grand and lofty the idea may be, no matter how vividly the picture may be painted, it can never be more than an idea, it can never be more than a picture. If, on the other hand, it can be shown to be practically workable from a governmental point of view, then it merely remains for the people, or rather, to speak more practically, the leaders in political thought throughout the Empire, to weigh calmly and dispassionately the advantages against the disadvantages of Imperial Federation, and to decide which has the preponderance. Unfortunately, however, it is difficult under our system of party government to set a new idea such as this in such a form as to be practically manageable. The question is so large, so broad and comprehensive, that it is impossible so to present it as to appeal to the ordinary intelligence and feelings of the great body of the electors. Considerable time must be required before such a general knowledge of the question is attained as to make it popular with the bulk of the people.

No political leader would care in the present unformed condition of public opinion to adopt 'Federation of the Empire' as a party cry. The risk to his party would be too great. Even to identify himself prominently with the question would be dangerous, as, until the matter is more thoroughly understood, it is much more easy to stir the small and narrow feelings of a multitude against federation than it is to convince the higher and noble reason in favour of it. We can imagine how the popular demagogue on the eve of an election would inveigh against the candidate who was favourable to federation of the Empire. Trembling with patriotic zeal, he would denounce the man who would ' destroy the grand old historic Parliament of England,' who would ' suck the life-blood of the country ' by a system of national emigration, who would ' rob the taxpayer' of England by making him pay the interest on the Colonial debt, together with much else of the same sort, calculated to rouse the venom of an unthinking crowd. And yet the federation of the Empire is a question of the highest and most supreme importance to the nation. If the reasonings and deductions of the foregoing pages have any truth in them at all, the most vital processes of the national life are ultimately dependent on the answer to be given to this question. Neither is it a matter that can be very long delayed. The rapidity with which the Empire is developing will soon place the matter beyond the realm of discussion, and the form the question will soon assume will be, not how to retain the Colonies, but how to regain them. It has already been shown that the natural development of the Colonies can only result in separation from the Mother Country; there would seem to be no escape from this. Under the present Colonial policy the position to which every Colony is moving is that of complete separation from the Mother Country, and it is only a matter of time when the political organism of the Colony shall have sufficiently developed itself to bring about this result. But, apart from the separation that must ultimately and certainly be thus effected, there is the probability of the separation being brought about earlier through secondary causes. A glance at the course of recent Canadian politics will show this.

As most readers of the 'Westminster Review' probably know, Canada has adopted a protective tariff. At the general election for the Dominion Parliament, which took place in the autumn of 1878, the Conservative party, led by Sir John A. Macdonald (then in opposition), adopted the protection cry in order to carry the election. Canada, like every other country, suffered from the recent depression in commercial circles. Protection was prescribed by the Conservative party as the nostrum that was to cure all commercial ills. Adopt a 'national policy' that will exclude the manufactures of other countries; foster and encourage Canadian manufactures by the imposition of a prohibitory tariff; keep 'Canada for the Canadians,' and, said the Conservative party, all will be well. Under these doctrines the people were taught to believe that the importation of cheap manufactures from England was an injury rather than a benefit. The fact that a man could purchase cloth imported from England more cheaply and of a better quality than he could make it in Canada was, instead of a matter for congratulation, a matter full of danger to the well-being of the people. Exclude the English cloth by a high tariff, and force all to use the worse and the dearer, and one step towards commercial prosperity will have been gained. No matter how subversive of reason and common sense these arguments may seem when thus nakedly stated, yet when dressed in election garb by the skill of the demagogue they had the effect of winning over the great body of the electors to the Conservative side. As the result there is now established in Canada a strongly protective tariff. Let us trace the consequences of this.

The British manufacturer finds that under the new tariff he is unable to trade with Canada as formerly. While, on the one hand, as a British taxpayer, he is required to assist Canada by guaranteeing the payment of the interest on Canadian loans, on the other hand he is by the Canadian Government denied the privilege of trading with Canada. Naturally this results in a feeling of irritation, and representations of the injustice committed are made through the press and otherwise; while it is pertinently asked, 'If the Colonies turn against us in this manner, why continue a connection so humiliating?' To the Canadian the matter presents itself differently. He has been taught to believe, and no doubt does believe, that the admission of British manufactures is an injury to his country. He feels that it is of the utmost importance to him to 'secure the home market.' He feels that his material interests are bound up in this protective tariff; that with this tariff his commercial prosperity must stand or fall; and if the result of this should be to endanger British connection, then 'so much the worse for British connection.'[1] Thus, we see on either

[1] As stated in the *Toronto Mail*, the leading Conservative newspaper of Canada.

side of the Atlantic a feeling is produced which is antagonistic to the maintenance of the connection between the Mother Country and the Colonies, and which might possibly, at any moment, cause a disruption of the union. Clearly the only way to obviate such difficulties in the future is by the adoption of an uniform fiscal policy throughout the Empire, and by the adoption of such a system of Imperial governing as will render it impossible for any one part of the Empire to legislate against another part.

It must be borne in mind, in dealing with this question of federation, that it is not so much the present that should be considered as the future. Though, as the foregoing pages have shown, the Colonial part of the Empire is by no means unimportant either in population or wealth, yet this is but the germ of the future Empire. In attempting to forecast what will be the growth within the next fifty years, one cannot but be amazed at the vastness of the figures. The population will probably be not less than 70,000,000, and may be very much more. Is England content to let this vast Empire slip from her grasp? Is she content to contemplate herself in the future as confined to the narrow limits of the British

Isles? When she has been able, by the power of her arms, by the heroism of her soldiers, by the energy and endurance of her sons, to acquire and develop these vast countries, is she not also capable of the still grander effort, and by widening her political system, hold them all under one supreme sceptre? Upon the answers given to these questions depends the future of the British Empire. If the present policy be persisted in, the result is easily foreseen—the British Empire will be broken up, and England, burdened with immense debt and vast responsibilities, will be left only with those Colonies that are too small and unimportant to be able to separate from her. On the other hand, if the political system of England be expanded and broadened so as to embrace all the Colonial possessions, there will be established an Empire that must in the future rule the destinies of the world. Which shall it be?

POSTSCRIPT

In the sixteen years that have elapsed since the foregoing was written, the net result has been a strengthening of the feelings holding the Colonies to the Mother Country. The Colonies have not, however, increased in population, nor has their trade grown to the extent that then seemed probable. Particularly is this the case with Canada. This checking of growth is doubtless due to the extraordinary fall in the value of agricultural products the world over, which has rendered the life of a Colonial settler much less attractive ; and also to the adoption of heavy protective tariffs by the Colonies in general, which have increased the expenses of the farmer, while his profits have diminished. Still there has been a definite growth in the population and wealth of each Colony, and the day is brought so much the nearer when the size and importance of the Colony will be such that the demand for full national life will be irresistible. It cannot be supposed that a spirited and energetic people, when grown to the size of a nation, will be content to remain a Colony. They will desire—and rightly desire—to have a proper voice in the supreme affairs of their national life. For Canada to obtain this voice three possible courses lie before her—federation with England, annexation to the United States, or independence. Annexation is a mean-spirited idea that the great majority of Canadians reject. By it Canada would sell her birthright, and much that is noblest and best in her life, for a very unsatisfactory mess of pottage. The national burdens thrown upon her would be out of all proportion to the national status that she would attain by the change. Independence would place Canada in the position of a fifth-rate Power living by the sufferance of the neighbour to the south of her. The expense, too, of maintaining even a moderately-adequate army and navy would put a very heavy burden on the country. The noblest destiny for Canada is federation with England. When the cravings for national life become so strong that they must be satisfied, it is to be hoped that the political system of the Empire will have been so expanded as to allow of the admission of Canada—as well as other Colonies—to a share in the direction of national affairs. The time will surely come when the people will be aroused to a sense of the inferiority of the Colonial position, and will demand a voice in the supreme affairs of the Empire; when they will ask that they should share the responsibilities, privileges, and burdens of national life. It is to be hoped that, when that crisis in the life of Canada arises, England may be able to grant the request that will certainly be made.

GRANVILLE C. CUNINGHAM, F.R.C.I., M.I.C.E.

MONTREAL: *July* 29, 1895.

www.ingramcontent.com/pod-product-compliance
Lightning Source LLC
Chambersburg PA
CBHW020114170426
43199CB00009B/532